"*Mrs. Oswald Chambers* is a lively biography of the woman behind *My Utmost for His Highest*. That famous devotional book probably owes as much to the skills and dedication of Biddy Chambers as it does to Oswald. The story of how it came to be (years after Oswald's death in Egypt) is interesting, and so is the faithful, trusting, and attractive life of the woman who produced it."

> Tim Stafford, author of more than thirty books
> including *God's Justice: The Holy Bible*

"A deeply engaging and luminous introduction to the life and love story of a remarkable woman. The details included in *Mrs. Oswald Chambers* left me feeling as if I'd spent a memorable afternoon sitting beside this 'Beloved Disciple' to whom an entire generation of devotional readers are indebted. Inspiring and beautifully crafted."

> Robin Jones Gunn, bestselling author

"Oswald Chambers has been a dear friend and spiritual mentor to me over the years. What a delight to get an inside look at the man—and woman!—behind my favorite book, *My Utmost for His Highest*. Biddy Chambers' willingness to use her gifts for God's glory brought Oswald's words to the world. Her faithfulness in the midst of sorrow challenges me today. Thank you for this important new book!"

> Joanna Weaver, bestselling author of *Having a Mary Heart*
> *in a Martha World*

# Mrs. Oswald Chambers

The Woman behind the
World's Bestselling Devotional

## MICHELLE ULE

### BakerBooks

a division of Baker Publishing Group
Grand Rapids, Michigan

Published by Baker Books
a division of Baker Publishing Group
PO Box 6287, Grand Rapids, MI 49516-6287
www.bakerbooks.com

Printed in the United States of America

Library of Congress Cataloging-in-Publication Data
Names: Ule, Michelle Duval, author.
Title: Mrs. Oswald Chambers : the woman behind the world's bestselling devotional / Michelle Ule.
Description: Grand Rapids, MI : Baker Books, a division of Baker Publishing Group, 2017. | Includes bibliographical references.
Identifiers: LCCN 2017018731 | ISBN 9780801075148 (pbk.)
Subjects: LCSH: Chambers, Biddy, 1884–1966. | Chambers, Oswald, 1874–1917—Family. | Evangelists' spouses—Great Britain—Biography.
Classification: LCC BR1725.C43 U44 2017 | DDC 269/.2092 [B] —dc23
LC record available at https://lccn.loc.gov/2017018731

Scripture quotations are from the King James Version of the Bible.

All quotations from *My Utmost for His Highest* are taken from the classic edition.

The author is represented by Books & Such Literary Management.

17  18  19  20  21  22  23      7  6  5  4  3  2

With gratitude to all who have encouraged, loved,
and taught me in my Christian walk:
teachers, pastors, Bible study members,
authors, and praying friends

As well as
my children, grandchildren, and husband

And
to the memory of
Biddy and Oswald Chambers

*Soli Deo Gloria*

# Contents

# Prologue

*Faith and Experience (November 13, 1908)*

How can anyone who is identified with Jesus Christ suffer
from doubt or fear?[1]

The cathedral loomed as they exited the tube station into a
crisp November morning in 1908. Gertrude Hobbs's blue
eyes twinkled at Oswald Chambers from beneath her black straw
hat as she took his arm. "You want to show me St. Paul's?"

The morning light shadowed his high cheekbones. "Have you
been here before, Beloved Disciple Biddy?"

She loved to hear him use his new nickname for her. "Of course
I have."

He patted her hand. "There's something new inside I want to
show you."

They strolled past the booksellers' warehouses to the western
face of England's "mother church." The cathedral sat on the highest spot in London and showcased the city's tallest spire, pointing to
God. Twenty-four broad stone steps brought them to the entrance.

The morning was a gift; they had so little opportunity to spend
time with each other. Their affection had developed during a

ten-day voyage to America, a few quick visits in New York City, and many exchanged letters. Biddy had quit her job in New York and returned to England because of his words.

Finally reunited, they only had the weekend in London. Oswald would leave within days to speak at League of Prayer meetings in Ireland, northern England, and Scotland. They didn't know when they'd meet again.

Written words sustained and nourished their hearts, always, but that Friday morning Oswald directed Biddy to an oil painting not far from the glorious dome. She'd read about it in the newspaper. "The sermon in a frame?"

Holman Hunt's painting "The Light of the World" depicted Jesus dressed in kingly robes in a dark garden, a lighted lantern in one hand, the other stretched to knock on a humble wooden door without a knob.

Revelation 3:20 had inspired the painting: "Behold, I stand at the door, and knock: if any man hear my voice, and open the door, I will come in to him, and will sup with him, and he with me."

Evangelists recognized the painting as a clarion call to show how Jesus awaits invitation into each person's heart. Oswald indicated the crown of thorns Jesus wore, and they discussed the painting before he explained why he wanted her to see it.

Oswald needed Biddy to understand that if she married him, their home would be meager, with their lives "going heart and soul into literary and itinerating work for Him. It will be hard and glorious and arduous."[2]

Biddy knew marriage to Oswald would not be a relationship focused on each other. God's call commanded Oswald's time and attention. She viewed her role in partnership with him and God as a helpmeet—a woman specifically designed for Oswald's needs and God's purposes.

Her beloved painted no romantic pictures. Indeed, Oswald cautioned, "I have nothing to offer you but my love and steady lavish service for Him."[3]

Captivated by her faith in God and the man before her, Biddy agreed. Before the Hunt painting, Oswald and Biddy promised to follow God's lead together and to give their utmost energies to accomplish God's highest plans.

But what kind of woman would accept such a challenging proposal?

# 1

# Discovering Divine Designs

## *1883–1907*

Never allow that the haphazard is anything less than God's appointed order.[1]

The fog would gather quietly in the moist winter night above London's Thames River. Born of cold air, the murky cloudiness would deepen and thicken as it moved over the water toward land. It would then crawl up the riverbanks north and south and cloak feeble gas streetlamps struggling to push back the dark.

As dawn broke and the sun rose, the fog and coal smoke mixture—first called "smog" in 1905—would turn yellowish brown with a smoky, acidic smell. For young and old people suffering from inflamed lungs or fragile hearts, the sooty particulates swelled air passages and gripped chests.

One such winter's day in 1895, the smog wisped through the massive Royal Arsenal walls ten miles east of Big Ben on the Thames. It drifted by the Royal Army barracks and slipped along

Woolwich's narrow streets to a townhouse set behind a flower garden: #4 Bowater Crescent.

The smog's microscopic particles slid under the door and found twelve-year-old Gertrude Annie Hobbs. Her lungs seized into air-sucking spasms.

She struggled to climb the stairs to the bedroom she shared with her sixteen-year-old sister, Dais. Her congested chest weighed heavy, and she could not catch her breath even when she lay down. Weariness plagued her, and schoolwork, even the literature she loved, blurred into bewilderment. Gert closed her aching eyes to rest, yet her mind raced.

At first her mother thought Gert must have caught the type of cold virus most people endured in a Victorian England of sodden handkerchiefs and close rooms. In an era before antibiotics and asthma inhalers, effective treatments were limited. Emily Hobbs plumped up her daughter's pillows, steamed the room with a boiling kettle, and prayed.

Henry Hobbs returned from the gas works that evening and stared at his youngest child, her wan features a mirror of his exhaustion. Her rattled breathing and dark-circled eyes troubled him. The son of a master baker, Henry had seen many men laboring to breathe flour-choked air in the bakery kitchen. His own father gasped for breath a mile away in his home on Powis Street.[2]

They called the doctor. Tapping on Gert's chest and listening, he diagnosed bronchitis, a viral inflammation of the lungs now known to be exacerbated by air pollution.

Physicians in the 1890s prescribed opium or morphine for bronchitis, along with an expectorant to clear the lungs. Emily fed her child wintergreen drops to soothe the searing coughs. She pushed her lips into a reassuring smile as she listened to Gert's wheezing and watched the girl's red-cheeked attempts to take a deep breath.

Eleven thousand people in greater London died of bronchitis in 1895.[3]

But not Gertrude Annie Hobbs.

The smog eased in the spring when household chimneys belched less smoke. Migrating birds returned, flowers pushed through the warm soil, and Gert's lungs cleared. She returned to school behind in her studies. Nineteenth-century teachers emphasized rote memory work, which made it harder to keep up outside of class, but in her quest to be perfect, Gert tried.

The blue-eyed girl with wavy dark hair who had languished during the winter months blossomed in the summer as she played tennis with Dais and their mother. She resumed piano lessons, cavorted with the family dog, and rode her bicycle in nearby Woolwich Commons. The family sang hymns around the piano in the evenings. They read aloud and laughed together. The tension eased from Henry's shoulders and Emily set aside her fears.

A cheerful woman, Emily Hobbs combined her fondness for entertaining and playing tennis by hosting frequent tennis parties. Emily handled the cooking and baking while employing a live-in teenage servant to help with the rough work. Like her daughters, she cherished books and, thankfully for all, Woolwich boasted several lending libraries. While deeply in love with her hardworking husband, Emily delighted in her three clever children: Edith Mary (called Dais—short for Daisy), born in 1879, Herbert (called Bert), born in 1881, and Gertrude (called Gert), born in 1883.

The Hobbs children grew up during the final two decades of Queen Victoria's reign. Bowater Crescent rang with cadences from the nearby barracks and the hoofbeats of military and civilian mounts headed south to Woolwich Common. Soldiers attached to the Royal Regiment of Artillery frequented the neighborhood as they marched to the Royal Arsenal.

The 150-acre Royal Arsenal stretched for a mile along the Thames waterfront. Tons of coal smoke poured from its lofty smokestacks as thousands of employees manufactured armaments and performed weapons research. Not long after Gert's birth, an explosion at the arsenal sent rockets flying up to two miles away.

Woolwich residents ignored such dangers. The town's fortunes rose and fell with the Royal Arsenal, which provided the necessary income—whether at the arsenal or in related industries—for the seventy-five thousand people living in the area.

And yet the arsenal's industrial smoke mingled with the deep fog each fall and winter. When this smog enveloped the town in 1896, Gert's lungs clamped down again. Feeling as if iron boots weighted her chest, she returned to bed. Fever took hold, her airways narrowed, and Emily ran for the kettle.

Gert spent her time reading—Robert Louis Stevenson's stories were favorites—and trying to keep up with her studies. She recovered in the 1897 spring, but her bronchitis roared back again in the fall.

Concerns for Gert's health intensified in October 1897 when Henry's father died from asthenia—exhaustion compounded by respiratory issues.[4] Emily and Henry watched their daughter carefully. She might outgrow the bronchitis, but it often led to pneumonia. With Gert's weakened lungs, tuberculosis could set in—always a concern in the nineteenth century. In 1900, 407 people died of either bronchitis or tuberculosis in Woolwich.

Despite her efforts, Gert fell too far behind in school. Her parents removed her for good in early 1898. She was fourteen.

Girls of Gert's social class generally finished school at sixteen, often to prepare for marriage. Gert, however, preferred to follow Dais's example. The close-knit sisters wanted to marry someday, but for the immediate future they aimed for success in the working world.

Dais took to heart her mother's fears of financial ruin and pondered her father's faltering health and long working hours. When she neared graduation, Dais applied herself to the skills necessary for office work—the most acceptable alternative to teaching for women on the cusp of the twentieth century.

At five feet, five inches, a tall woman for the time, Dais stood ram-rod straight with narrow, sloping shoulders and a tightly corseted waist. With straight dark brows above blue eyes, she wore her curly brown hair knotted on top of her head. Precise and efficient, loving and generous, Dais doted on her mother and encouraged her sister's dreams.[5]

With the same height and bright blue eyes as Dais, Gert had a rounder face and dark hair that often escaped its hairpins into tendrils. She never showed her teeth in photos and her trim figure resembled her sister's, though she was not as tightly corseted.[6]

As the miserable 1897–98 winter slipped into spring and Gert's breathing eased, her restless mind, denied school, sought another outlet. Gert wanted to help the family, a desire made imperative by her fifty-year-old father's failing health. Her family history—particularly on the maternal side—underscored the reason for concern.

Raised by Woolwich master baker Samuel Hobbs and his wife, Mary Whiteman Hobbs, Henry was the oldest of three sons. The whole family worked in the bakery (Mary behind the counter), but Henry did not want to be a baker.

Emily Amelia Gardner, meanwhile, grew up in Gravesend, the youngest of six children of master baker George Gardner and his wife, Ann Whiteman Gardner. Ann Gardner was Mary Hobbs's sister, making Henry and Emily first cousins.

The Gardner household once employed servants but, by Emily's birth, an embezzling business partner had destroyed the family's standard of living. George Gardner's 1866 death scattered his family into poverty and forced Emily to move in with a widowed cousin's family in London. At age sixteen, she became little more than a servant.[7]

By the 1871 census, twenty-one-year-old Henry worked as a clerk in a Greenwich church. It's not clear when Henry and Emily first fell in love, but their parents did not approve of their proposed marriage, possibly because they were cousins. Kathleen Chambers later surmised the families disliked the disparity in their social situations, which, combined with Emily's longing for financial security, may have been the catalyst for Henry's ambition and hard work.

By the time of his 1875 elopement with Emily, Henry worked as an auctioneer. Shortly thereafter, he took a position as a commercial clerk—a midlevel accountant—to provide Emily with the lifestyle she craved.[8] As Henry advanced in the Woolwich gas works, they moved from rented rooms to a leased townhouse on Bowater Crescent, cementing their advancement into the middle class of Queen Victoria's day. Emily settled into her happy life.

But Henry Hobbs died suddenly on June 18, 1898, three weeks before Gert's fifteenth birthday. His death certificate listed the cause as "cerebral atrophy and exhaustion," the equivalent of a stroke in modern medicine.

Her husband's death devastated Emily Hobbs. She lost her emotional, financial, and personal support in one cruel blow, far too reminiscent of her father's catastrophic death.

Henry had rescued her from "poor relation" status with their marriage, and Emily cherished their life. While he left a comfortable estate, the 2015 equivalent of $220,000, the inheritance would require careful management to sustain the family—particularly Emily—for the rest of her life. And Emily did not have the training for such a task.[9]

Dais stepped into the financial gap and went to work as a clerk in a money-order office of the British postal service. Bert found a clerking position at the Woolwich gas works. The family released their servant and took in a boarder. The women shared cooking, cleaning, and laundry chores.

Gert finally outgrew her bronchitis, though she sustained permanent hearing loss in her left ear. Determined to contribute to the family finances as well, she signed up for a Pittman Shorthand correspondence course. Times were changing. The Royal Arsenal had hired its first four female typists in 1895 (out of some fourteen thousand workers), and accomplished female stenographers could find employment in the business community.[10]

Gert quickly mastered the basic components of shorthand: hooked dashes and curved marks differentiated by their width and placement on a line. Similar to learning a foreign language, the more she practiced, the less she needed to "interpret" the sounds into symbols on the page. Her fingers soon automatically responded and penciled shorthand into a notebook.

Dais and Emily helped her practice. Using a yellow Dixon pencil, Gert placed the sharpened lead on the left-hand side of the paper and, listening carefully, wrote in a fluid motion whatever Dais or Emily read aloud. Once Gert "took down" the passage, she read it back to check for accuracy. Her ability to decipher her notes without error demonstrated her mastery of the skill. Gert always strived for perfection in everything she did; she sensed a path to future success with stenography.

An 1895 article in the *Manchester City News* noted salaries would double if a woman possessed two skills, as "the rates of pay testify to the desirability of making typewriting and shorthand go hand in hand . . . it is essential that girls who desire to become typists should be well up in English composition—spelling and correct punctuation being indispensable. They must be business-like, neat, attentive, accurate, and loyal to their employers."[11]

And so, as soon as she mastered shorthand, Gert turned her nimble, piano-playing fingers to a boxy black typewriter and learned how to touch type. Her goal? She wanted to be the first female secretary to the prime minister of England.

Once confident in her abilities, Gert applied for a job at the Woolwich Royal Arsenal. Hired as a typist, the diligent Gert got along well with her employer and colleagues, especially another typist her age named Marian Leman.

With her children gainfully employed, Emily managed the household and dealt with her grief. Their boarder, Reverend Charles Hutchinson, may have encouraged her faith and membership in a local Baptist church.

Emily spent her free time reading and studying the Bible, praying, and having friends in for tea. Her faith grew even as the family's financial circumstances changed. At some point after 1901, Reverend Hutchinson left Woolwich, Bert moved out, and the women had to seek a smaller home.

They relocated to #38 Shooter's Hill Gardens on Westmount Road, a few miles south in Eltham. Built of brick on the flanks of Shooter's Hill (the highest elevation in Kent, with views to London), the new two-story row house boasted a small garden facing the wide street. They could walk to the shops on nearby High Street and to local parks.[12]

Dressed in fashionable white shirtwaists and dark skirts with straw hats perched on their heads, Dais and Gert would catch public transportation to their Woolwich jobs each morning. Despite being in their early twenties, neither woman had marriage prospects on the horizon.

Emily Hobbs transferred her Woolwich church membership to the newly formed Eltham Park Baptist Church down the street. Her daughters joined her, and the three women participated in the ministries and services held at the simple hall.[13]

Eltham Park Baptist Church's first pastor preached his first sermon on Easter Sunday, 1904. The Reverend Arthur C. Chambers had come to the fledgling congregation from a nearby Baptist church. Under his pastoral leadership, membership quickly grew to 140 worshiping in the service and 150 attending Sunday school.

Emily's warmth and hospitable nature overflowed to church members. Sunday afternoon tea provided opportunities for further fellowship and their cozy home soon filled with new friends.

Gert's spiritual life remained private; she never spoke of giving her heart to Christ or professed any sort of testimony. Yet, throughout her life, anything that caught her interest received full exploration. She studied the Bible and memorized the psalms. After her many disappointments, the loss of her father and the dissolution of their home, the psalms brought comfort.

Dais remained equally silent about her faith. The two sisters applied for church membership at Eltham Park Baptist Church within the year. They were baptized together by immersion at the October 29, 1905, evening service. Gert was twenty-two, Dais twenty-six.[14] Their overjoyed mother wrote her "darling girls" a letter commemorating the event:

> My heart is too full for me to say all I should like to you both, it is full of joy at the step you are taking today, a step that will brighten and influence all your life. May that dear Savior. . . . Be very near to you and may you realize the strength of the promises. . . . It makes me so happy to see you both working for the Master.

In the letter, Emily also referenced her disappointment that Bert showed no interest in God. She urged her daughters to pray for him. Her final words were those of a doting mother:

> God bless you darlings for all your loving thoughtful care for me, bless you in all your undertakings, ever guide, guard, comfort and strengthen you, and give you much joy in His service. So prays your very loving Mother.[15]

Emily couldn't have suspected her prescience the day she penned her letter. Gert's first step into service to God became a lifelong walk in obedience and sacrifice.

Shortly after the happy baptism, Reverend Arthur Chambers's youngest brother came to Eltham to lead a weeklong mission during the Christmas holidays. With a budding reputation as a galvanizing and learned lecturer for the interdenominational League of Prayer, Oswald Chambers spoke nightly on how to be yielded to the Holy Spirit.

The six-foot-tall man who addressed the congregation that December was in his early thirties. Angular and lanky with deep-set blue eyes and brown hair swept from a receding hairline, Oswald Chambers relished opportunities to talk about Jesus Christ, the Holy Spirit, and God himself.

Genial, with a playful sense of humor, and gifted with words, he talked quickly and with an intensity that captured his listeners' attention. Oswald lectured extemporaneously, without notes. His only goal: "To have honorable mention in somebody's life in introducing them to God."[16]

All three well-read Hobbs women appreciated the depth of his teaching. For Gert, his sermons provided opportunities to practice her stenography skills; she listened and learned better when her hands were engaged.

Emily naturally invited the visiting preacher to the house for tea, no doubt thinking such a godly man must be in want of a good wife.

And with such invitations to tea continuing from Emily, Oswald Chambers visited the family whenever he filled in for Arthur. An articulate guest full of stories and a lover of literature and God, not to mention music, hymns, and dogs, Oswald felt at ease in the Hobbs home.

He was not, however, seeking a wife.

The seventh of eight children born to devout parents in 1874, Oswald spent his early childhood in Scotland and northern England. The family moved to London in 1890. As a teenager, he accompanied his father, Reverend Clarence Chambers, to hear Reverend Charles Spurgeon preach at London's Metropolitan Tabernacle. Oswald gave his life to God that night.

Notably talented in music and art, Oswald played the organ, trained at London's Royal College of Art, and returned to Scotland in 1895 to study art at the University of Edinburgh. He also pondered theology and visited local churches to hear the accomplished preachers then occupying Edinburgh's pulpits.

He saw himself as a bridge between intellectuals and God. Oswald anticipated his love for literature, music, and art, along with his devotion to the gospel, would surely touch a chord in the lives of sensitive artists.

Jobs and income, however, did not materialize. Eventually Oswald came to the reluctant conclusion God might be calling him to the ministry. Despite feeling far from God at the time, he enrolled at Dunoon Bible College near Glasgow in 1897, where Reverend Duncan MacGregor, founder of the small college, mentored him.

God finally breached Oswald's dark spiritual period during a 1901 meeting of the local League of Prayer, where he claimed the gift of the Holy Spirit as a result of Luke 11:13: "If ye then, being evil, know how to give good gifts unto your children: how much more shall your heavenly Father give the Holy Spirit to them that ask him?"

As part of the Holiness Movement then sweeping the British Isles and America, the League of Prayer focused on an individual's personal salvation and how to apply God's moral law to behavior. Oswald appreciated the League's focus on prayer, church revival, and the spread of biblical knowledge—which corresponded to God's emphasis in his own life.

The League, which operated one hundred centers around the British Isles (including thirty in London alone),[17] sponsored more than thirteen thousand services in 1897. It also published a monthly magazine, *Tongues of Fire* (later retitled *Spiritual Life*), for which Oswald occasionally wrote. League of Prayer founder Reader Harris recognized and encouraged Oswald as a promising speaker and teacher. Shortly after meeting the Hobbs family in late 1905, Oswald became a volunteer circuit lecturer with the League.

He received no salary and lodged with League of Prayer members in the towns where he spoke. Offerings and personal gifts covered his train fares. The lack of a salary didn't bother Oswald—he believed

God would provide for all his needs and had ample experience of him doing so.

Oswald soon became friends with Japanese evangelist Juji Nakada. He traveled to America with Nakada in November 1906 to teach a course at God's Bible School, which was affiliated with the Holiness Movement, in Cincinnati, Ohio.

Afterward, the two journeyed to Japan, where Oswald examined international evangelism and missionary work. He resumed speaking for the League of Prayer when he returned to England in late 1907. (Upon his return, Oswald pulled a coin from his pocket to show his brother and pointed out he had traveled around the world on a mere shilling!)

As the years went by, Oswald concentrated his thoughts on God rather than on seeking a wife. A teenage romance had brought joy and anguish, leaving him reluctant to invite a woman into his nomadic ministry life. Oswald served God better unencumbered. He didn't have the income to support a wife, much less a home.

Loved by dogs, children, old ladies, and members of the League of Prayer, Oswald was welcomed everywhere by Christians who wanted to advance the kingdom of God. His relationships remained cordial with no suggestion of anything beyond good fellowship.

And so his friendship with the Hobbs women proceeded amiably for two and a half years—until one day, when Emily Hobbs wrote him a letter.

# 2

## The Spontaneity of Love

### 1907–8

Love is not premeditated, it is spontaneous, i.e., it bursts up in extraordinary ways.[1]

*W*hile Oswald traveled the world teaching about God, Gert advanced in her career at the Royal Arsenal, possibly working in the commanding general's office. As one of sixty thousand female office workers in England at the time—4 percent of the clerical population—Gert proved a proficient and capable secretary.

The British prime minister still did not have a female secretary in the early twentieth century.

Home life in Eltham continued with church activities and the usual rounds of tennis, bicycling, walking, and laughing with her family and her friend Marian.

A petite woman with dark hair and a charming smile, Marian Leman grew up in northern England. She moved in with a sister living in Woolwich about 1900. As her friendship with Gert grew, she visited the Hobbs household regularly for Emily's teas and received invitations to attend religious activities with the family.

By 1907, her Methodist lay preacher father feared Marian had become "too religious," perhaps owing to the Hobbs family's influence. In hopes of redirecting Marian's enthusiasm, Frederick Leman sent her to Brooklyn, New York, to visit a cousin for the summer. While there, Marian met stenography teacher Edward Moore. She returned to England in the fall and then rejoined her Brooklyn cousin—and Edward—in spring 1908.

Not long after her 1908 arrival in Brooklyn, Marian wrote suggesting Gert join her. She had a job lead for Gert in a law office. Gert liked the idea and purchased a second-class ticket on the SS *Baltic*, set to sail in May.

Middle-class young women did not commonly sail alone across the Atlantic to an unknown job in 1908. Gert left no record of why she elected to travel to New York. Perhaps the nearly twenty-five-year-old wanted an adventure or a new challenge? Perhaps international experience might bolster her résumé, should the prime minister seek a new secretary?

While Emily Hobbs supported Gert's unexpected opportunity, she felt relieved to hear Reverend Arthur Chambers's brother Oswald also planned to travel to America in May on the *Baltic*.

Reminding him of the friendly afternoons with the family, Emily wrote to ask a favor. Since he was sailing on the same ship as Gert, would he mind looking out for her?

Oswald had planned his voyage to New York as a needed oasis before the busy summer camp season in Ohio and New England. He already had a box of books to read while relaxing in a deck chair. He wanted to rest and watch the wonder of the sea—but now the widow Hobbs had asked him to tend her daughter.

He knew Gert as the quiet one, an attractive girl with thoughtful eyes, always scribbling on a pad of paper. She asked intelligent questions and didn't simper or demand attention. It would cost him little to be of assistance and to put Mrs. Hobbs's fears to rest—though why was Gert sailing alone to New York?

He replied to Emily with assurances he'd watch out for Gert on the voyage.

Gert journeyed by train to Liverpool to board the enormous White Star Line ship. She carried her suitcase, sixteen dollars (US $396, 2016),[2] and every expectation of a God-directed and exciting future. As to her mother's arrangement with Oswald Chambers, a man nine years her senior, Gert shook her head. If it made her mother feel better, fine. She considered him a kind, wise teacher, but nothing more. She never imagined there could ever be anything between the two of them beyond simple friendship.

Oswald met the young woman at the ship in Liverpool as promised. He escorted Gert to meals and talked with her at the table. Oswald always appreciated good conversation.

As they savored the blue hues of the shallow Irish Sea and then the deep Atlantic Ocean, they discussed their similar tastes. They both loved poetry, Sir Walter Scott's books, and God. They shared friends in common. She played the piano, loved the countryside, liked to walk, and adored hymns and dogs—just as he did.

For the weary itinerant preacher, an intelligent Christian woman who listened closely and asked nothing of him must have been refreshing. His interest sharpened as they dined in the long saloon hall or sipped tea. Soon their conversations moved beyond the superficial into deeper subjects.

While Oswald undoubtedly spent time wrapped in a rug on a deck chair as planned, he set aside his books or at least shared them. For ten days, without pressing engagements, lectures to give, or trains to catch, he relaxed. Oswald could watch the sea and listen to Gert's calm voice. Time to get to know someone well must have been pure joy.

In her, Oswald discovered a young woman who understood his passion for serving God and who recognized the importance of prayer. Gert didn't require an explanation for the League of Prayer.

When, since his teenage years, had he spent so much time with an interesting and pretty woman?

Gert, for her part, felt no reservations talking with such a charming and trustworthy man of God. Limited in experience to the Woolwich environs and London, Gert asked about his travels and ministry, not to mention his previous trip to America. Within days, they felt comfortable confiding in one another.

When she shared her reasons for traveling to New York on the *Baltic*, they both must have wondered if the God they worshiped had his hand in the timing.

Perhaps with Oswald Gert felt the burden of her family's past heartaches lift. She could talk about her late father and describe her baker grandparents and their experiences as tradespeople—the very type of people who flocked to hear Oswald speak in England's industrial communities.

As a man without personal financial resources, Oswald's ears pricked up when she spoke of the family's adaption to their living situation with aplomb and success.

Gert's practical response to her school-ending bronchitis must have impressed him. She didn't abandon hope or her dreams because of a "mere" physical problem. With God's help and the talents he gave her, Gert turned what could have been a dreambuster into an opportunity.

Gertrude Annie Hobbs was not a weak woman who required coddling. She knew how to care for a home, could bake, and possessed secretarial skills along with a merry spirit for adventure. Her clever sense of humor made him laugh.

Oswald became more intrigued. Certainly he had noticed her taking notes when he spoke at Eltham Park Baptist Church, but he didn't realize her extraordinary ability.

He may not have known that any good stenographer could take down shorthand at 120 words a minute—or as fast as a person spoke. He must have been impressed, however, when he learned Gert's speed: 250 words per minute.[3]

28

Perhaps he volunteered to help her practice by reading while she took down shorthand, but at some point an idea stirred. Speakers and clergymen often hoped to write books. Regarded as a compelling devotional speaker, Oswald himself thought the most lasting preaching of all came from the pen. What caught his attention first—the idea of working together or her personal qualities?

Oswald often nicknamed the people in his close circle, and this became crucial in this case as this young woman with watchful eyes shared a name with his favorite sister, Gertrude. He recognized the young woman at his side embodied 1 Peter 3:3–5, with her "meek and quiet spirit, which is in the sight of God of great price" (v. 4). He knew of Gert's devotion to Jesus.

"How about 'Beloved Disciple?'" he asked.

Gert could hardly disagree, but "Beloved Disciple" soon proved to be a mouthful. Oswald shortened it to the initials B. D., which morphed into "Biddy."

The nickname stuck, and that was who she remained for the rest of her life. Even Emily and Dais adapted to the new name.

Gertrude Annie Hobbs knew Oswald to be a respectable man of God; could his obvious reluctance to leave her side during the day mean something more than a favor to her mother? With this new nickname, Biddy must have wondered about opening her heart to the possibility of this new friendship being more than a voyage-long camaraderie.

Wherever the discussion of themselves and God took them, not to mention their prayers about this surprising attraction, once they arrived in America on June 5, Biddy and Oswald had to part company. They exchanged addresses and went their separate ways, both astonished they had fallen in love.

As Oswald later wrote to his parents: "I am in love and it is quite such a new experience that it opens up so many unknown things that I do not know quite how to put it."[4]

Reunited with her friend at the docks, Biddy stayed with Marian in her cousin's Brooklyn flat on Rugby Drive. She took the subway into Manhattan to work. "She loved working in America," her daughter said many years later. "She thought it was absolutely wonderful because the bosses came in before she did and they worked hard all day long. When it came time to stop work, everybody went home. She loved being in America."[5]

The two English women thrived that summer. When it got too muggy, they could eat ice cream and visit Coney Island's Luna Park near the cooling shore. The Brooklyn Dodgers baseball team played in Washington Park. Theodore Roosevelt's presidency commanded the newspapers even as reporters buzzed about the Republican nominee for the fall election, William H. Taft.

In addition to the sights, Biddy and Marian shared confidences about the older men who had captured their hearts—Marian and Edward Moore were smitten with each other too.

Few of the letters between Oswald and Biddy survive, but their written words began in 1908 America. With Biddy newly pressed into his heart, Oswald wrote daily and she responded in kind.

An inveterate correspondent, Oswald filled his letters with descriptions of nature, references to spiritual truths, and warm affection. He often included inside jokes and quotations from the books he read. He described his talks at God's Bible School camp meetings and the gracious hospitality he received everywhere.

In Oswald's letters, Biddy learned his priorities: God, people, nature. She responded on the same subjects and described the novelty of the new world, her discussions with Marian and Edward, and her experiences working with the curious American spelling.

Oswald taught at the camp meeting in Cincinnati from June 19 to 26. He then traveled to North Attleboro, Massachusetts, thirty miles north of Providence, Rhode Island, where he spoke for nine days starting on July 3. On the way to Massachusetts, his train stopped in New York City, providing him an opportunity to see Biddy.

After North Attleboro's meeting, he continued north to Old Orchard camp near Portland, Maine, where he stayed for a week. Early August found him again in New York. He then sailed for Liverpool on the *Baltic* (which regularly crossed between Liverpool and New York) on August 4, returning to speaking commitments with the League of Prayer.

Before he left America, Oswald wrote to Biddy: "All in His good time we have the love, thank God, and the discipline of our characters alone or blended, it is all in His hands."[6] Oswald and Biddy always sought to follow God's hand at work in their lives. A ten-day voyage, three months of letter writing, and two hurried visits in Brooklyn had sealed their understanding of God's unexpected change to their personal plans.

Perhaps they had only intended to visit America for the summer— though unlikely, given Biddy's need to earn a living—but Biddy and Marian returned to England together in late September. They sailed on the *Baltic* out of New York, sharing a second-class compartment. Arriving in Liverpool on October 2, 1908, both women listed their occupations on British immigration forms as "none."

Maybe no occupations but plenty of plans and dreams filled their hearts and minds. While crossing the Atlantic, Marian received a telegram from Edward Moore asking her to marry him. She responded with one word: "Yes." They wed in Brooklyn on March 26, 1909.

Biddy probably found employment once she returned to England. Nothing had been decided—yet—but God's direction clearly pointed toward a future with Oswald Chambers.

Shortly after his return to England, Oswald wrote Emily Hobbs, asking if she had any objections to his writing to "Gertrude." Emily asked him to clarify his intentions: Did he mean a platonic friendship?

As a traveling preacher with little money, Oswald had no place to lay down his head, but, he explained, "I certainly do not mean 'Platonic' . . . but I do mean a friendship with view to an engagement and ultimate marriage."[7]

Emily smiled and sent her blessing.

Oswald knew his father would question his ability to support a wife. The League of Prayer had extended his time as a missioner, not a paid employee. He didn't know when he could wed. He wrote to his parents:

> My call is still as strong as ever. "Go ye into all the world and make disciples of all nations" and I will go, and ultimately I expect Miss Gertrude A. Hobbs will go with me. I cannot yet conceive what good I can be to any woman . . . yet I am sure His hand leads.[8]

Oswald and Biddy had a strong and practical faith. God brought them together. He would make their steps clear.

The only question was when.

# 3

## The Secret of the Lord

### 1908–10

It is God who engineers circumstances.[1]

On Friday, November 13, 1908, Oswald escorted Biddy to St. Paul's Cathedral in London.

He wasn't nervous; he had her mother's blessing but he wanted to see Biddy's face as he spelled out the challenges of marrying him. They both knew he could never be completely hers, because first and foremost he belonged to God.

Oswald expected the same of Biddy.

The enormous seventeenth-century cathedral stretched wide arms into the Ludgate Hill neighborhood, beckoning all to hear the good news of Jesus Christ. Even then, the boys' choir sang from ancient carved stalls behind the high altar, their sweet voices soaring into the expansive dome designed by Sir Christopher Wren. Oswald loved the music and art found in the glorious cathedral.

Now he led Biddy to a specific piece of art newly hung the previous June: "The Light of the World." The life-sized depiction of Jesus drew crowds to the cathedral for months.

After they discussed the painting, Oswald gave her an opportunity to count the costs of an alliance with him: "I have no prospects, just God."

But she loved him—his mind, his heart, his commitment to their God come what may.

"I don't know when we can marry. We must tarry until God opens the way," Oswald said.

"I'll wait."

A joyous Oswald presented her with a simple ring set with three tiny diamonds. They were engaged.

That night, the two attended a meeting at Speke Hall, the League's headquarters. Founder Reader Harris prayed for Oswald at the end of the evening: "Lord, take him to Scarborough, and Ireland, and Scotland, and bring him back to us laden with souls."

"It has been a royal blessed day," Oswald wrote in his diary that night.[2]

With Harris's prayer ringing in his ears and Biddy's love tucked in his heart, Oswald left London to travel nonstop for the League of Prayer. During the lengthy trip to Ireland, Scotland, and northern England, he wrote Biddy every day.

The November stay in Belfast introduced Oswald to a fascinating woman, Katherine Ashe, who lived at the same boardinghouse. Nearly ten years older than Oswald[3] and a confirmed agnostic, the tall, thin, and severe Miss Ashe (as everyone always called her) sniffed at the thought of a League of Prayer teacher. She couldn't imagine what they would talk about and expected him to be appalling.

Miss Ashe tried to argue with him over the dinner table, in a "glorious clash," reported Oswald in a letter to Biddy. He conceded to Miss Ashe that he knew nothing as important as Jesus Christ and "apart from Him, God was a mere mental abstraction."[4]

Miss Ashe blinked in surprise. Perhaps she had underestimated him.

She adored music and literature, and Oswald amazed her with his knowledge in those areas—he not only knew classical composers but could play them on the piano. He loved poetry and Ibsen's modern dramas; he maintained a gracious, friendly, and polite demeanor.

All the lodgers' hearts warmed to Oswald, and they attended one of his lectures out of courtesy. At this particular talk, Oswald felt compelled by the Holy Spirit to make an altar call, something he rarely did. To the astonishment of her friends, the proud, aristocratic lady in a black dress walked slowly from the back of the hall to the front as a sign she'd given her life to God.

Miss Ashe took her change of heart seriously. Years later she described the experience as being "a wholly supernatural conversion . . . a very agonizing birth from above," followed by "an intensely painful period of readjustment of every point of view . . . to honorably accept the New Testament standard."[5] Despite being the daughter of a clergyman, Katherine Ashe needed to read and study her Bible with new eyes. She applied herself to the task immediately.

Oswald cheerfully welcomed Miss Ashe into the body of Christ. A week later, he moved on to Scotland.

His letters described his experiences on the lecture circuit: "I speak and people get blessed, but I long to hear them say—'He made me love Him better.'"[6] Oswald shared his dreams so Biddy could know his thoughts, pray about his circumstances, and understand their expected life together in God's service. She could also read about his lectures in the newspaper or the League's publication, *Tongues of Fire*.

Oswald's affection for Biddy ran deep, as demonstrated by his response to a teasing letter from Emily Hobbs in 1909: "Hungry for Biddy? I think I'll run the risk of eating her up when I see her. God bless her. She knows something of how I love her."[7]

None of Biddy's letters to Oswald survive.

It may have been at this time that she went to work for a barrister near central London's Covent Garden. Legal work provided Biddy with valuable training for the future Oswald envisioned. Office management, accounting, correspondence, and organizational skills filled her days. Her work could have no errors, which suited her insistence on perfection. By typing up legal documents all day (including counteroffers and corrections using legal language) and taking down all the back-and-forth of negotiations, Biddy learned the nuances of contract management.

In March 1909, their marriage plans became even more problematic when Reader Harris unexpectedly died of a stroke. Harris's death meant more unpaid preaching and teaching roles for Oswald. He accepted the task.

As the new leader of the League of Prayer, Mrs. Reader Harris passed increased responsibilities on to her daughter Mary (always referred to as Mrs. Howard Hooker). Oswald watched the two formidable women assume leadership and wrote to Biddy about their future partnership: "I can see how mightily God will use us as one."[8]

Later that month, Oswald acknowledged his wish to spend more time with Biddy, but the ministry took him back to America in 1909. Oswald sailed on the RMS *Lusitania* that June to teach once more at God's Bible School and other summer camps. Upon arrival, he visited the newlyweds Marian and Edward Moore in Brooklyn. He wrote an encouraging postcard to Biddy and then caught a train to Cincinnati.

Living with and ministering to people at the summer camps reminded Oswald of boarding with the MacGregor family at Dunoon and the changes he saw when people spent concentrated time together studying the Bible. Prior to his voyage, he'd discussed with League of Prayer members the idea of a Bible training school where resident students could learn how to teach the Bible. Oswald's experiences in Japan examining how best to train missionaries motivated his enthusiasm—along with the opportunity to work with Biddy at his side.

The camps reinforced his enthusiasm for a future dream: he and Biddy living in a house "with a big garden where people could come and be at ease and find God and be healed of all the things that distressed them and worried them."[9]

As he wrote his intended,

> My whole soul is full of thoughts and prayers and waiting and working for what God is preparing for us in the near future. My idea of a Bible Training School for about ten years will yet come about. Four years—the country. Four in a city and two in a foreign field. Keep these schemes in your mind and heart.[10]

Biddy knew how to work hard, run a household, and cook. She always delayed personal gratification to put others first. God had called her to marry Oswald, thus she submitted her life to God's direction.

Later, Oswald wrote, "I realize . . . if we are not to forgo the interests of His cross, we must forgo a great many other interests . . . counting Him worthy of the cost."[11] Everything in Oswald's life turned to Jesus and the cross. As he later advised, "no matter how many things seem to be pressing in on you, be determined to push them aside and look to Him."

Biddy recognized the importance of her skills; more than once Oswald wrote, "I want us to write and preach; if I could talk to you and you shorthand it down and then type it, what ground we would get over! I wonder if it kindles you as it does me!"[12]

Why not? She might never be the prime minister's secretary (he didn't hire a female secretary until World War I), but she could be a helpmeet to a man whose passion matched hers: service to

God. Later, she would recognize Oswald's remark as a charge to her entire life.

Oswald returned to England in August 1909 and resumed the League of Prayer lecture circuit. The leadership pondered the League's next steps; they liked Oswald's Bible training college idea but weren't prepared to open a school yet. Instead, the League proposed Oswald create and teach a six-month Bible correspondence course.

He readily agreed and constructed a syllabus: eight individual assignments mailed to the students to complete at home. Students had two weeks to write their answers to his questions and return the lesson by mail. After a week—in which Oswald graded the coursework—the students received the corrected papers and the next lesson.

Three hundred students enrolled for the first term of the Bible School Correspondence Course.

In addition to directing the course and correcting papers, Oswald maintained his rigorous speaking schedule around southern England, including several lectures a week at London's Speke Hall, which Biddy could attend. This hectic winter brought with it a promise from the League, however: a May 25 wedding date. Biddy could finally make plans.

While Oswald still was not receiving pay, apparently the new leaders Mrs. Reader Harris and Mrs. Howard Hooker had concluded it was time for their primary speaker to be wed. As the League leadership prayed and made plans for a Bible college, they undoubtedly recognized Biddy's skills as an administrator. A live-in college could provide both room and board for the couple without the League having to pay Oswald to teach. Whether their decision came from romantic or pragmatic reasons is unclear; the ministry needed Oswald, and marriage would make him happy.

Why wouldn't Oswald demand payment for his exhausting work? Some might argue from 1 Timothy 5:18: "the labourer is worthy of his reward." Oswald, however, like many devout Christians of the nineteenth century, viewed money as a potential distraction from ministry.

Among the concepts he may have discussed with Biddy while standing in front of "The Light of the World" was:

> Jesus never had any home of His own, never a pillow on which to lay His head. His poverty was a deliberate choice. We may have to face destitution in order to maintain our spiritual connection with Jesus, and we can only do that if we love Him supremely.[13]

Believing God would provide for Oswald and Biddy's needs in accordance to God's plan was a core value to him. "We have to trust in God whether He sends us money or not, whether He gives us health or not. We must have faith in God, not in His gifts."[14]

While Oswald received gifts from people who heard him speak, all his personal needs were met as he traveled around the British Isles. Such a situation suited him well—he wanted his trust to be in God, not the coins in his pocket.

Along with everything else on his plate that spring, Oswald managed to write his fiancée regularly, seeing with clear eyes what their marriage would mean: "This union is His and He will look after you and me. All we have to do is obey and work and love."[15]

Years later he wrote to a friend, "When I think of [Biddy] I can but look into the face of God and say in my soul, 'God is good.'"[16]

Oswald sent five pounds (about US $600, 2014)[17] to Emily Hobbs two weeks before the wedding to help with expenses: "Please accept it as a token from a son to a mother. Your imagination is not all taken up with losing a daughter is it? Because you are gaining a son."[18]

In other letters to his prospective mother-in-law, he spoke of Biddy as a treasure while having misgivings of himself as a husband. Biddy had no such doubts.

The sun shone bright as the bridal party made their way to Walford Green Memorial Wesleyan Methodist Church in Eltham. The Reverend Arthur Chambers conducted the ceremony.

Oswald's League of Prayer friend from Dunstable, Percy Lockhart, stood up with him as best man. The groom wore a stiff white clerical collar and a black frock coat.

Arthur's daughter Doris carried roses as the flower girl. Gertrude Chambers, looking as angular as her brother, served as a bridesmaid, and Dais attended her sister as maid of honor. Gertrude and Dais wore similar high-necked dresses trimmed in lace with narrow, corseted waists and wide-brimmed black hats decked with flowers. Doris, too, wore a large hat, which was white and tied with a neat bow beside her left ear.

Biddy's brother, Bert, looked elegant in a morning suit as he escorted her down the aisle past a beaming Emily Hobbs and Oswald's parents, Clarence and Hannah Chambers. Carrying a flowing bouquet of May roses, Biddy took careful steps in her long-sleeved, high-necked, lace-covered white gown.

She didn't wear a hat or a veil in the sole wedding photo. She faced the camera, her brown, curly hair pulled back with escaping tendrils ringing her calm face.

The new couple held a small reception in the garden of a nearby Baptist parsonage. The long wait was finally ended; their life together had begun. Several days later, Mr. and Mrs. Oswald Chambers boarded the SS *Coronia* in Liverpool for a ten-day honeymoon voyage to America.

They landed in a hot and muggy New York on June 7. Oswald settled Biddy with Marian and Edward in Brooklyn, mailed three hundred graded papers to England, and caught a train to Cleveland. In returning to God's Bible School camps, he taught an American version of his correspondence course. Oswald repeated the exercise—reading and grading hundreds of papers—eight times over the course of the summer.

Biddy joined him in July for a week of just the two of them at Thomas Seifferth's Meadow Lawn house in the Catskills' Plattekill Valley. As Biddy later wrote, the scenery "left us with the sense of worship expressed by Isaiah, 'the whole earth is full of his glory.'"[19]

While the Catskills week refreshed them before the push on to other camp meetings, Oswald dictated at least one article and maybe an entire book to his new wife during that time. Biddy, of course, already knew her husband worked to his utmost for God's tasks.

As she traveled with him to camp meetings for the rest of the summer, she met people from Oswald's past, including missionaries to Japan Charles and Lettie Cowman at the Denton, Delaware, camp. She also befriended the Hittle family when they hosted the Chambers couple at their Ohio farm.

The honeymooners finished the summer at the National Holiness Camp in Old Orchard, Maine. After another short stay with the Moores in Brooklyn, they caught the SS *Adriatic* home to Southampton.

Ahead of them lay more League lectures, more correspondence studies to correct, and a new career.

# 4

## Building for Eternity

### *1911–12*

As workers for God we have to learn to make room for God.[1]

*W*hat passed through Biddy Chambers's mind as she surveyed the restless sea and the enormous sky while lounging on an SS *Adriatic* deck chair with her husband of four months at her side?

He wore his hat low over his brow and a blanket covered his legs. Focused on his book yet conscious of her presence, Oswald glanced up occasionally to meet her eyes and smile. He craved the relaxation he always found at sea. No one knew him on board ship; he could recharge his energies for the future.

If Biddy sought adventure, Oswald and God provided it during their travels. The successful camp meetings overflowed with enthusiastic people seeking and finding God's holiness in worship and teaching. Biddy and Oswald had traveled as far south as Maryland, as far north as Maine, and as far west as Ohio. Biddy took shorthand notes the entire time. They lived out of their suitcases and rarely slept more than a few nights in the same place.

She had traveled vicariously through his letters during their engagement but now she experienced Oswald in action. The man did not slow down. If not preaching, he was preparing to preach or grading papers. His extroverted personality greeted everyone he met, and money flowed through his pockets—in generosity to the needy—as soon as God put it there.

Most importantly, he thought prayer the greater work and he prayed continually.

As she got to know her new husband through their prayers together, Biddy delighted in his heartfelt requests. Oswald reviewed and prayed over his lengthy list daily. Acting as a mere messenger, he longed for people to seek and find their sanctification in God alone.

Biddy had counted the costs of loving Oswald. Their honeymoon only confirmed her devotion to him; he inspired her even more than he inspired his listeners. Deeply in love, she rejoiced as the man she adored shared God's truth with lost souls and confused saints. Traveling with Oswald as he spoke for the League of Prayer would provide even more opportunities for rejoicing—and taking shorthand.

While Oswald and Biddy honeymooned in America, the League of Prayer leadership prayed and planned for the prospective Bible college. Under "occupation" on his September 29, 1910, British immigration papers, Oswald wrote "college tutor." Biddy listed herself as "wife."

Biddy had looked forward to long conversations with Dais and their mother around a teapot upon her return to England. Once reunited, however, Mrs. Chambers only had enough time to catch up on family news, do the laundry, inspect the mail, and pack again. Another travel adventure beckoned. Life with Oswald presented the world.

Following the correspondence school's success, the League made arrangements for Oswald to teach the course in a circuit around northern England. Oswald still managed his students by mail, but in addition would teach the same class on Tuesday nights in Stoke-on-Trent, Thursday afternoons and evenings in Blackpool, and two Saturday sessions in Manchester. He'd preach in local churches on Sundays and conduct evening League of Prayer meetings.

Papers needing to be graded would arrive as usual. In addition, he'd have Biddy with him on this trip. League of Prayer members knew Oswald from his previous swings through the countryside. They were curious to meet his wife.

In Blackpool, on the Irish Sea, Oswald always lodged with William and Anne Docking, along with their two children, Bill and Dorothy. Nine-year-old Dorothy eagerly awaited Oswald and his bride. As she considered Oswald a type of handsome fairy prince, Dorothy's expectations soared. Surely he had married a golden-haired, blue-eyed fairy princess with pink cheeks?[2]

No.

Worse, Dorothy didn't think Biddy looked noble enough to have married her prince.

But as the girl got to know Biddy, she loved her—dark hair, laughter, confident personality, and all. Like Oswald, Biddy told stories, knew tricks, played the piano, and sang. The Chambers couple together charmed Dorothy.

The first night in Stoke-on-Trent, Biddy picked up her pencil for the beginning of her public ministry in England. She traveled with Oswald, prayed for him, and at every lecture sat in the back and took down everything he said word for word. Biddy also typed up her notes—important for when he needed to review the lectures for other classes. She managed their personal correspondence and kept their relatives informed about their plans.

Fortunately, Biddy's responsibilities did not extend to the correspondence school. That task, particularly the mail, fell to a trusted woman who spent her life serving Oswald and God: Oswald's favorite sister, Gertrude.

Like Biddy, Gertrude Chambers had been desperately ill as a child and was not expected to live. Tall and lanky and only two years older than Oswald, Gertrude outgrew her illness. But while her sisters Bertha, Florence, and Edith worked as dressmakers' assistants or children's nurses, Gertrude remained in the family's top-floor flat in the London suburb of Dulwich.

Unsung Gertrude, number one on the Rye Lane Baptist Church roll for seventy years, served her God well. Her final pastor described her as "a very strong character, always ready with some pithy comment. [I] got the impression she was like Oswald. To her, he was a wonderful interpreter of the mind of Christ and she spoke of him with the utmost love and respect."[3]

When Oswald needed someone to handle the correspondence school's mail, Gertrude volunteered. The task enabled her to take part in something important to the kingdom of God even as she cared for her frail and strong-willed father, Clarence, and sweet mother, Hannah. Converted by Charles Spurgeon as a young man, Clarence Chambers preached about a harsher God than his son. For him, God showed no mercy, no gentleness. (Clarence was "utterly humorless," according to Kathleen Chambers.)[4]

More than once Gertrude had to coax him down from preaching while standing on a trunk in his nightshirt: "Father, for goodness' sake, this is the end of the day," she'd say. "Just get back into bed and go to sleep."

And Clarence would answer, "No. Sit down and listen to the Gospel."[5]

Gertrude picked up the correspondence course mail, repackaged it, and sent it to Oswald's latest address. A week later he returned the corrected papers, signing them with a red-inked rubber stamp reading "Oswald Chambers." She folded in the next lesson, stuffed each one into a hand-addressed envelope, and mailed it back to the students.

One hopes Clarence appreciated reading the lessons himself. Cheerful Hannah undoubtedly relished the letters her son and daughter-in-law always included in the package.

Oswald's course that fall was biblical psychology, which examined the theology of the soul and was based mainly on the first chapters of Genesis. From those passages, Oswald discussed humanity's relationship to God and provided biblical answers for moral dilemmas. Students loved the course and clamored for more.

Meanwhile, the League of Prayer leaders prepared to open a Bible training college. The Harris and Hooker families lived in mansions near London's Clapham Common, a convenient mile from League activities that centered at Speke Hall. When a magnificent townhouse nearby became available in December, the League rented it and announced the college's opening in one month.

Biddy and Oswald, the grandchildren of bakers, a blacksmith, and a Thames waterman, caught a bus to the address and stood in the gravel courtyard looking up at #45 Clapham Common, north side. Their eyes rose higher and higher as, with open mouths, they studied the six-story-tall, five-townhouse-wide building. Hidden from the avenue by a line of fragrant cedar trees, the Cedar Terrace townhouses displayed enormous splendor.

All five townhouses featured balconies on the second and fourth levels. Carved stonework marked the other floors and the roof line. Ivy-covered walls hiding the light-colored granite met above the arched doorway of #45.

Oswald and Biddy climbed seven steps to a black double door with shiny brass knobs under a fanlight. Inside the entry hall, a wrought-iron bannister accompanied sweeping stone stairs all the way to the top floor, ninety-six steps up. A previous owner's colorful coat of arms emblazoned the first landing window. On the second floor, Oswald and Biddy opened mirror-paneled doors into a drawing room spanning the building front to back. They glanced at each other. Had either one ever seen such a room outside of a museum?

Mrs. Howard Hooker, no stranger to wealth and a neighbor at #38, thought the drawing room looked "almost too magnificent for a lecture hall."[6] Halfway down the drawing room and facing each other on both sides, gilt mirrors hung over two ornate fireplaces. Marble pillars in the corners supported a colorful Italian scene depicting maidens, cherubs, seraphim, and winged heads painted on the ceiling. Gold leaf covered the background and molding while polished parquet floors completed the room's opulence.[7] French doors opened to the southern balcony and views to the 220-acre Clapham Common. The northern windows overlooked a private garden and a private lane.

The couple climbed through the house from attic to basement with eyebrows raised in wonderment at its nineteen rooms. The bedrooms upstairs featured marble fireplaces and more decorated ceilings. They never dreamt of such a place for a college.

While laughing at the costly touches, Oswald and Biddy didn't forget the reason for the awe-inspiring mansion. They paused in each room to pray God's blessings on the college, the people destined to stay in the rooms, and those God would bring through the doors. The greater work began before the initial students ever heard of the BTC—as they now referred to the Bible training college.

"We're spoilt bairns of the Almighty,"[8] Oswald said as he closed the front door.

Such an overwhelming provision for a couple who owned no household goods fit Oswald's expectations that God always provided whenever and wherever he led. It was another example of why Oswald never worried about money.

With plans to open a coeducational college in four weeks, the League leaders invited friends interested in the new venture to attend a reception. After showing guests through the empty townhouse, they asked for financial gifts as well as physical donations of furniture and necessary accoutrements. Mrs. Howard Hooker used the resulting funds to purchase iron bedsteads, "institute" chairs with a right arm that folded to form a small desk, dining room furniture, and kitchen equipment. Her enthusiasm for the BTC knew no end and she always treated the college as a pet project.

Biddy received the role and title "lady superintendent." Her responsibilities included running the household, managing the books, handling correspondence, and overseeing the servants and students. The cook shopped and cooked, but Biddy supervised.

The League hired Arthur and Alice Morrison, a general manager and a cook who had once worked at another house in the neighborhood, as household staff for the BTC. They moved into the basement with their three young children and a teenage nursemaid. The BTC eventually used five servants, who were also part-time students. Anyone associated with the school or the League was welcome to attend classes or prayer times.

The BTC provided dormitory space for up to twenty-four residents; the lecture hall accommodated seventy students and the dining room seated fifty. Oswald and Biddy probably took the front bedroom on the third floor above the lecture hall.

Mrs. Reader Harris held the title of BTC president, with Mrs. Howard Hooker as secretary and her solicitor husband, Howard Hooker himself, as treasurer. In 1914, the BTC patrons included nine clergymen and one woman ("Mrs. T. H. W. of Pelham").[9] With no endowment beyond prayers, in keeping with Oswald's stated preference, the school held only sufficient funds to meet the expenses a week ahead.[10]

The lady superintendent put faith into practice running the school's household. Living with Oswald's confidence made it easier. They prayed for funds; God provided them at the perfect time.

The League of Prayer held opening ceremonies on January 12, 1911. When Oswald rose to speak, he confessed himself overwhelmed God included him in such a wonderful program. The school's motto: "For Christ's Crown and Covenant."

During the first term, the curriculum centered on classes Oswald had already taught: "Biblical Psychology" and "Biblical Ethics: The Moral Life." The latter dealt with the importance of Christ's atonement in a person's life and how to apply the ethical principles to behavior. It made a natural progression from learning the theology of "Biblical Psychology" to actually applying it.

Oswald arranged the class schedule to make the college accessible both for students living in the house and for men and women who could attend only one lecture per week. Visitors could ride the tube to Clapham Common Station, a ten-minute walk away, or take the Cedars Road electric tram.

As superintendent, Biddy handled all the smallest details, including making up beds for new students and supervising the Morrisons—a new experience for her. At the time of the April 1911 census, only one student lived in the BTC: Violet Richardson.

Those first months, Violet alone dined in the elegant dining room with her principal and superintendent. Oswald believed biblical truth was more easily "caught" than "taught," particularly in learning to serve one another. Unfamiliar with a life attuned to the ways of God, Violet studied the Bible over the next two years but also learned how to apply its truth to her own life.

Violet was the first in a long line of women who sought Biddy for counsel and friendship. Always willing to make time in her busy day and share a cup of fragrant tea, Biddy listened and prayed with simplicity. Oswald's and Biddy's sympathetic ears attracted hurting people, as Oswald had foreseen. Throughout their lives, people confided in them—knowing they never betrayed a trust.

Violet may have been the sole resident, but part-time students from the community joined her during the BTC's first term. The classes met in the glorious lecture hall, now outfitted with a wheezing pump organ and a large blackboard.

Oswald taught his biblical psychology course at three other locations in London that spring. He continued his correspondence school with double the number of students from the previous fall. (With up to six hundred students writing eight different papers, there would be over three thousand essays to grade, giving that red stamp plenty of use.) With Dulwich only four miles away, Gertrude Chambers easily visited and provided assistance as needed.

Indeed, they saw family regularly, particularly as Dais and Emily Hobbs now lived in the neighborhood.

With Biddy no longer contributing to the household, her mother and sister closed up the Eltham house. Dais had advanced in the Civil Service and may have transferred to a spot closer to London's government buildings near Parliament and Big Ben. By April 1911, possibly earlier, the two lived with the Claylands Congregational Church pastor and his family in rooms a short distance from the BTC.

Her mother's presence may have helped Biddy as she adjusted to her new role. Having well-loved women with whom she could pray, confide, and swap clothes provided a haven of familiarity. Besides, with Dais gone all day and few housework chores, sixty-one-year-old Emily needed something productive to do in the afternoons. Tea with the Bible students suited her perfectly.

When the semester ended in late May, the college closed for three months. Oswald spent the early summer speaking at League of Prayer meetings, where Biddy dutifully took down his lectures in her notebook. In August, Oswald and Biddy traveled on holiday to one of his favorite places: the ancient village of Askrigg in the hills south of the Scottish border. The countryside in what is now Yorkshire Dales National Park boasted emerald pasturelands separated by stone walls, with windswept limestone crags towering above. Sheep dotted the hillsides and streams flowed through valleys—called "dales"—to the River Ure. In the early twentieth century, Askrigg had a population of less than five hundred, and Oswald first visited as a guest of his League of Prayer friend Major John Skidmore, a local clockmaker's son. Oswald especially loved the irony of a fifteenth-century stone church dedicated to St. Oswald at the village crossroads.

Oswald and Biddy rode the Great Northern Line railroad over a quaint stone bridge to the cobblestoned village, where they stayed in a tiny room across from the church. In the clear air and empty countryside, Oswald rambled for miles through rugged fields and heather-filled moors. He hiked for hours without seeing another soul, savoring the bullfinches' high-pitched calls and startling black grouse into flight.

When joined by Biddy, the treks involved a picnic—they boiled potatoes over a fire and ate them "in heaven's dining room." Wildflowers covered the hillside, and Oswald fished to his heart's content in the icy streams, while Biddy read nearby. With a sky full of constantly changing light, the dales spoke of God's handiwork in motion and a time to rest in the natural world they loved.

Rest for Biddy, however, differed from relaxation for Oswald. The man taught a Bible study each night in their lodgings. On Sundays, Oswald preached at local chapels and visited friends in nearby Wensleydale—often with a local dog curled at his feet.

The days spent together praying, thinking, reading, and hiking in each other's company were a necessary pause before God answered Oswald's prayer for the school: "Send us more students, O Lord, until this place is filled with men and women through whom Thou canst glorify Thyself throughout the world."[11]

The BTC residence hall filled to capacity by the end of 1911.

Once the live-in students arrived for the fall term in late September, Biddy established a dining schedule. Group prayers began the day at 8:00 in the grand lecture hall. Breakfast followed fifteen minutes later, and dinner was served at 1:15. Tea, featuring a simple meal in addition to the hot beverage, came at 5:30, and supper at 9:00. The day ended with prayers at 10:00 in the lecture hall. In addition to encouraging guests at the evening classes, Biddy welcomed visitors and nonresident students at meals, where she set a vase of flowers in the center of the white tablecloth whenever possible.

A serious student of the Bible since meeting Oswald, Miss Katherine Ashe now appreciated League of Prayer meetings. Intrigued by Oswald's description of the college when he spoke at a September meeting in Belfast, Miss Ashe moved to London to join them. Most of the resident students, however, were younger than her forty-six years.

The twenty-four residents were generally evenly divided between men and women. They all participated and assisted in running the school and keeping it neat. Biddy posted a sign with a reminder of where their hearts should be in their tasks: "Notice: 'All service ranks the same with God.' You are requested to kindly do your part in keeping this room tidy. If you do not, someone else will have to.'"[12]

Male residents hauled coal and performed other heavy chores while women helped in the kitchen. Working side by side with the hired staff in fall 1911, several students soon grew concerned over the behavior of the house manager and cook.

Everyone noticed the lack of marmalade or eggs at breakfast, or when a roast vanished—according to Mr. Morrison—because of the students' appetites. However, a student soon approached Biddy concerning the disappearance of household items like blankets as well as food. "It's obvious who is doing this," the student said.

Lady superintendent Biddy checked on supplies and watched carefully. She was responsible for the couple's work. Uncertain of how to be fair to both the school and the Morrisons, she went to Principal Oswald for advice.

"Don't do anything," Oswald replied. "We'll tell God and leave it completely."

Biddy knew and understood her husband's reluctance to play the role of "amateur providence"[13] in the lives of others. She also knew that, for lasting change, the Holy Spirit needed to convict the couple's hearts, not her. The League and Oswald designed the BTC as a community for students to recognize God's truth in daily living with fellow believers, not to teach it explicitly. This life-application would be an opportunity for the students as well as the Morrisons. Not to mention the lady superintendent herself.

Biddy directed her surprised students to pray and say nothing.

When household items and food continued to disappear, she told the students to pray more. No one challenged the Morrisons. The house manager must have wondered how they were getting away with theft, but as Miss Ashe observed, the couple "were not used to living with folks who practiced" Jesus's Sermon on the Mount—"for where your treasure is, there your heart will be as well."[14]

The Morrisons noticed Biddy paid the housekeeping bills out of personal funds they knew she couldn't afford. They figured Biddy knew what they were doing but couldn't understand why she didn't complain to her husband.

First they mocked her innocence, then sneered, and finally shrugged. From toleration they moved to anger and resentment of the foolish woman who looked them in the eye and paid the bills they presented.

One day the confused house manager went to the principal to confess: "I am ashamed that my wife and I have been consistently taking things from your linen and store cupboards ever since your college opened. I can't bear the thought I have taken in you good people."

Oswald nodded. "You haven't taken us in. We knew you were doing it, but we wanted God's Spirit to tell you. I knew you would get convicted by God Himself for what you were doing, in His own way."[15]

Overwhelmed by the answer, Mr. Morrison "caught" what Oswald had designed the BTC to demonstrate: the Holy Spirit convicting of sin—thus enabling people to personally experience God's love in action.

Biddy grew in confidence out of this faith-building experience. She dismissed the repentant Morrisons but they left with grace and without rejection. The couple later submitted their lives to Christ.

The BTC required replacements, and a friend from Speke Hall, Mary Riley, stepped into the gap as the new cook.

The fourth child of twelve, Mary was the daughter of an Essex coachman who moved to St. John's Wood (a wealthy northwestern suburb of London) to work for a horse dealer. The family lived in a five-room home behind a spacious estate on Elm Tree Lane, not far from what is now Abbey Lane Studios.

Mary went into service, first as a nurse and then as a cook/companion. Her six sisters worked as dressmakers and her brothers were grooms in 1911. Plump, with dark hair and clear features, Mary was a few years older than Biddy. Her straightforward manner and splendid cooking skills drew thanks from everyone at the BTC. She attended classes when she could, as did several of her siblings.

Mary's friendship and dedication blessed Biddy her entire life, as would the love of others sent by God for reasons they couldn't imagine when they first walked through the BTC's front doors.

The most important one arrived in 1913.

# 5

# Vision

## 1913

It is the peril of our soul's welfare that we get caught up in
practical work and miss the fulfillment of the vision.[1]

*B*iddy and Oswald rose before daybreak each morning. They
brewed tea and read Scripture and that morning's *Daily
Light on the Daily Path* devotional together. Savoring the compan-
ionship over a cup of tea, the two would watch dawn's light spread
over Clapham Common—if the sun broke through the London
clouds that day.

Eighteen months into their marriage, Biddy had adapted to
Oswald's perpetual motion, and he appreciated her calm in the
midst of their demanding life. She'd learned to cherish these quiet
moments when they prayed together and discussed the day's plans
before Biddy dressed and swept off for the morning. Oswald would
continue with his preparations until just before eight o'clock, when
he descended to the lecture hall to pray with the household.

Everyone wanted a piece of her husband's attention and a moment of his time. Adored by rich and poor, old and young, seeker and satisfied, he remained remarkably grounded. Oswald ate each meal surrounded by eager students peppering him with questions while Biddy listened from the other end of the table. Who knew what the Holy Spirit would put in his mouth next?

It helped to know how ardently he loved her and that he recognized the challenges she faced as superintendent. His confidence encouraged her. Oswald often reminded Biddy she could handle the day's events if she kept her mind focused on God.

Oswald didn't know it when he wrote his letter in spring 1910, but his words then were perfect now and reflected his attitude toward his wife: "The Lord has been slowly rebuking me for wanting to shelter you. He is bringing me to understand this union is His and He will look after you and me. All we have to do is to obey and work and love."[2]

Biddy cherished his words—reflecting his concern for her personally—like a stone set within the ring of God's calling. Each morning she wrapped herself in his confidence and opened the bedroom door to a house full of diverse personalities and expectations.

The BTC overflowed with activity. Men and women alike were encouraged to attend, as: "there is neither male nor female: for ye are all one in Christ Jesus" (Gal. 3:28). As with the Morrisons, Oswald and Biddy expected the students to learn at their own spiritual rate and for the Holy Spirit to convict their souls.

Oswald began the school day at 8:00 by playing a hymn of praise on the lecture hall's pump organ. The students gathered in the sumptuous room to sing, read a portion of Scripture, pray a short prayer, and break for breakfast at 8:15. Each class during the day began with praise and prayer, and additional periods were set aside for group prayer throughout the week.

The school emphasized the importance of personal devotions, and students often gathered to pray for personal needs throughout the day. Oswald and Biddy encouraged them not to dwell on the prayer requests so much as to go right to prayer when they met. Oswald advised, "If you know too much you can't pray; the circumstances become so overpowering you are no longer able to get to the underlying truth."[3]

Prayer played a central role in all decisions. As Miss Ashe observed, "The BTC was born in prayer and cradled in prayer—and believing prayer was at all times its very life."[4]

A variety of teachers taught one-hour classes during the week. Mrs. Reader Harris began Monday morning with a course on Bible reading, Reverend James Douglas taught Greek classes for both beginners and advanced students, and Miss Ashe lectured on Christian sociology. Mrs. Reader Harris's younger daughter, Dorothea Harris, led a practical class on teaching Sunday school.

Students flocked to Mrs. Howard Hooker's Bible content class on Tuesday evenings. Using the lecture hall's blackboard, she would outline a specific book from the Old or New Testament with an overview of its contents. Oswald liked her blackboard outline method so much he used it for the rest of his life.

Biddy's Tuesday morning Bible memory class focused on precisely memorizing and accurately quoting Scripture references. She was a natural choice to teach the class with her determination to take errorless shorthand. Oswald loved to hear his wife speak and encouraged her to do so not only at the BTC but also for League of Prayer meetings. He thought her especially good with the psalms.

The rest of the classes fell to the principal himself and extended across many subject matters: Old Testament topics, Christian doctrine, Bible ethics, biblical psychology, Christian habits, and missionary matters. He prepared six lessons each week in addition to his correspondence course grading and League of Prayer commitments.

He set aside late Wednesday afternoons for a more personal devotional class limited to enrolled students. As most planned to be missionaries, he challenged them to examine God's activity in their lives. In particular, Oswald encouraged them not to allow circumstances to hinder their pursuit of God's plans. The students referred to it as "Spiritual Surgery."[5]

The sermon preparation class for the same group involved writing and delivering sermons. Oswald provided feedback.

With pencil and notebook in hand, Biddy attended every class and took down everything Oswald said. She filled a trunk with her notebooks.

Mealtimes were opportunities to discuss issues raised during class in further depth. Oswald often used his signature comment for confused or argumentative students: "Just leave it for now. Brood on it and it will come to you later."[6]

He always left his office door open for interruptions.

In addition to keeping track of the students and taking shorthand, Biddy bore responsibility for the smooth running of the household. She handled the bookkeeping—a challenge each week, as sometimes she had to wait for God to provide funds. When the black candlestick phone rang, she answered it: "Battersea 1270." Biddy read the mail and answered questions from prospective students. She often worked late into the night.

Mary Riley did the marketing and organized the student helpers into a work schedule. Her skills freed Biddy to handle the frequent task of dealing with visitors.

The BTC welcomed a broad array of Christian organizations to address the students, using lecturers as varied as Salvation Army officers or West London missionaries to discuss local opportunities. Oswald and Biddy also invited foreign missionaries from around the globe to describe the joys, difficulties, and triumphs of their work for the gospel. They wanted the students to gain an accurate picture of what missionary life entailed.

Biddy ran a ministry open to interruptions throughout her life, and this practice began at the BTC. Invitations to visit the school went around the world through friends. With League of Prayer members and Oswald's many acquaintances often stopping by, Biddy needed to be adaptable, no matter who arrived. Fortunately tea and soup could always be stretched.

Such resourcefulness served her well the day she opened the door to an unexpected telegram. A missionary from Africa's Gold Coast who was heading home to America on furlough was seeking a place to stay with his family for a week. A friend had suggested the BTC.

Biddy nodded.

The family of seven would arrive in two hours.

Her eyebrows went up.

She called a group of students to help. Four residents turned over their dormitory room and beds. Men hauled additional beds and furniture up the stairs and into place. Biddy phoned Mrs. Hooker about obtaining clothing for the family, preferably not worn hand-me-downs. She sent a student to the kitchen to let Miss Riley know she needed to stretch their meals.

Biddy realized busy London might overwhelm the children. Plucking coins from her purse, she dispatched another student to nearby High Street to buy small toys.

Once the family arrived, they heard the rest of their story. Born in remote Africa, the children had their first trip out of the "bush" on the ox-wagon journey to the coast where they boarded their ship.

The BTC residents enjoyed a week of fun and ministry. Biddy watched the children's wide eyes, solemn and amazed. "Everything was new, from a chair to a tramcar; from the ducks in the pond on the Common to the miniature airships for the boys to fly . . . every object was equally wonderful and strange," Miss Ashe recounted.[7]

As they bid the family goodbye from the doorstep seven days later, Biddy breathed a sigh of relief and gratitude before returning inside to await the next adventure.

Zulu native Brother Petros arrived one winter evening carrying only a small bag. Friends at God's Bible School in Cincinnati had given Brother Petros the BTC address and encouraged him to visit on his way home to Africa.

He related the tale of his Zululand childhood and the terrifying experience of being captured by Arab traders. Branded, beaten, and starved, Brother Petros escaped with a broken body. A missionary found him and, while nursing the young man back to health, presented the gospel message. Once healed, Brother Petros found a job in the diamond mines until he'd earned enough money to travel to America and study at God's Bible School.

Brother Petros wanted to share the good news with his people in their native language. He left the BTC covered with prayers and returned to a dangerous country. They never heard from him again, but his story of the difficulties and joy he felt in hearing and spreading the gospel inspired everyone.

The secret to Biddy's unflustered reactions to her lengthy to-do list and surprise visitors lay in her prayer time every morning. She gave God the day and watched it unfold in his timing with anticipation. But her composure also came from an attitude Oswald presented during that "Spiritual Surgery" hour in the form of questions:

> Are you willing to sacrifice yourself for the work of another believer—to pour out your life sacrificially for the ministry and faith of others? Are you willing to give and be poured out until you are used up and exhausted—not seeking to be ministered to, but to minister?[8]

Sitting in Oswald's classes, Biddy took down his words with her fingers but the concepts lodged in her soul.

The BTC ran two terms each year with three months off in the summer. Biddy and Oswald traveled for the League of Prayer once the 1912 recess began, this time with Biddy occasionally speaking also. The League recognized her gifts as well as Oswald's, and the couple poured themselves into teaching, praying, and talking with others. Biddy, of course, wrote down everything Oswald said.

August 1912 brought them the relief of Askrigg. They stayed in the same room above the Skidmores' shop, across the street from St. Oswald's Church, and hiked the hills. They had time to read, think, relax, and dream. Oswald fished to his heart's content.

They visited with friends, and Oswald preached on Sundays. Biddy's ministry of interruptions eased into a satisfying holiday of reflecting on God's goodness with like-minded believers, laughing over sheep filling the cobbled streets, and pondering what to do with free days.

The summer wind blew over the green countryside and cleared the London smog from their lungs. God's natural handiwork refreshed and cleansed their bodies and souls. When they returned to Clapham Common, Biddy was pregnant.

Back in the whirl of students, classes, schedules, prayer, bills, food, letters, and shorthand, Biddy swallowed the nausea and fatigue of early pregnancy. She modified her usual clothing—a white shirtwaist neatly tucked into a dark skirt—and loosened her corset. While she didn't have to go into the seclusion of Victorian times, women didn't flaunt or discuss their pregnancy in the early twentieth century.

Oswald adored children and felt beyond delighted. Emily Hobbs tried her best to fuss over her no-fuss daughter. With all the well-meaning women in the house, Biddy got plenty of assistance and sympathy. She kept up her busy schedule as long as she could, but the pregnancy proved difficult and she missed many of Oswald's spring lectures on the book of Isaiah.

After a difficult delivery, Kathleen Marian Chambers arrived on May 24, 1913, in the bedroom upstairs. The house rang with congratulations and thanksgiving for a healthy baby. As Miss Ashe wrote, "There was not one of us whose life was not touched by those baby fingers. She was a very bonnie, darling baby."[9]

Her infatuated father led the rejoicing.

During the Edwardian era, the "lying-in" period following child-birth lasted one month. The new mother spent the first two weeks in bed, followed by promotion to reclining on a bedroom sofa for week three. Biddy remained confined to her room during week four before being released to "light duty."[10]

Biddy's much-needed recuperation lasted from the spring term's end into the first months of summer. With Emily Hobbs undoubtedly and necessarily in attendance, she could relax, heal, and enjoy her cherished baby. She also needed to grieve. After Biddy's difficulties in the pregnancy and delivery, the doctor advised Oswald and Biddy to have no more children.

By August, Biddy and little Kathleen were strong enough to travel to Askrigg with Oswald.

Biddy didn't climb hills during their 1913 visit but could rest her eyes on the pastoral views and kiss her husband's flushed cheeks when he returned from a day outdoors. Everyone fawned over the baby and Biddy grew more adept at caring for her. By September and the start of the fall term, Biddy resumed her active life, albeit with Kathleen in tow.

Several students enrolled that fall to whom Biddy and Oswald grew exceptionally close. Welshman Philip Hancock, the oldest of twelve children, was specifically sent to the BTC by his missionary board to prepare for foreign mission work. In addition, one of Oswald's Yorkshire friends joined them in September. Twenty-eight-year-old Jimmy Hanson, a stout native of Denby Dale, had met Oswald and Juji Nakada through the League of Prayer, and after traveling the world he felt a call to the overseas mission field. The son of a shopkeeper and a bookkeeper, the practical Jimmy studied mechanics and engineering in school. Upon his return from New Zealand, where he worked repairing machinery, he enrolled at the BTC.

While originally designed to prepare people for the missionary field—no matter where or what their age—the BTC also accepted students with no such clear direction and provided a theological education and community life experience. Young women found a warm friend and mentor in Biddy, and daily interaction with Oswald meant they received nicknames.[11] Three such women in their twenties joined the community in 1913.

At twenty-two, Gladys Ingram, soon dubbed "Gladiolus," was the youngest of a dozen children. She grew up in Wimbledon, the daughter of a retired Indian barrister. Her brother was a missionary among the outcastes of India who had met Oswald ten years before through the League of Prayer. The willowy Gladys attended the BTC to explore becoming a missionary herself.

Sprightly Eva Spink grew up on a comfortable estate, the daughter of a Piccadilly fine arts dealer who received a royal warrant in 1900 to provide medals for Queen Victoria. Raised in a spiritually minded Plymouth Brethren home,[12] twenty-year-old "Sphinx" or "Spinkie" played the piano with a ready smile but was uncertain what she wanted to do with her life.

Kathleen Ballinger, "Bill," a comely beauty with dark hair, large eyes, and a mole on her cheek, arrived from Gloucestershire for a few weeks of "spiritual refreshment" and then decided she, too, had a calling to serve Christ.

One of the relationships that would be most important to Oswald and Biddy began in an evening class.

The director of a small publishing company bearing his name, Charles Rae Griffin stood as tall as Oswald, with shining blue eyes, a fair complexion, and a cleft in his chin. With two small children at home, he and his wife, Norah, attended class only one night a week. Hearing Oswald's lectures seared "Radiant" Griffin's soul. "I knew that I had at long last struck reality. Having done so, how to share it with others?"[13] (The Griffins later named their youngest son John Oswald.)

As the vice-chairman of the Council of the London Baptist Missionary Union, Griffin requested a copy of Oswald's talks to share with friends. Biddy provided typed copies, and he made arrangements to have them printed (though not through his company, which specialized in technical journals).

His friends snatched up the pamphlets. Griffin charged a small sum to cover costs and the booklets became known as the Discipline series. He designated any profits for student scholarships at the BTC.

Various magazines, most notably the League of Prayer's *Tongues of Fire*, printed Oswald's sermons from time to time, and the leadership of God's Bible School in Cincinnati particularly appreciated his correspondence course. When their publishing house, Revivalist Press, inquired about publishing Oswald's notes on biblical psychology in 1911, Biddy typed them into an orderly form and mailed them.

Revivalist Press published *Biblical Psychology* as a book in 1912 and Oswald obtained copies to use in his correspondence course. The American publishing house did the same with his *Studies in the Sermon on the Mount* in 1915.

Thus began Oswald's dream of lecturing, with Biddy taking down his words, and then seeing the lectures published into pamphlets and books.

Their life flowed beautifully as God provided everything Oswald had dreamed: a residential Bible college, Biddy as a partner in ministry, people eager to learn about God, and an adorable baby.

Kathleen flourished in the BTC's loving environment. When Oswald required Biddy for dictation, she handed her infant to a cooing friend and slipped into the lecture hall. Women clamored to hold the baby, play with her, bathe her, and feed her. Men stopped to run a finger down her soft cheeks and, always, her father fawned over his child.

Charming, confident, and full of chatter, Kathleen walked in good time from encouraging outstretched arms to enchanted kisses. Emily Hobbs and Dais visited frequently.

Even austere Miss Ashe couldn't contain herself, describing Kathleen as "a very vocal Baby, and she led us at prayers and on

Sunday afternoons in a way distinctly her own—if it did thrill some of us with the thought of those words about 'perfected praise.'"[14]

But while well appreciated, all the attention concerned her parents. As a traveling Oswald wrote to Biddy:

> Remember, Kathleen is God's gift to us, not someone we give to God. Do not allow the influence of the many loving women around you to turn your heart away from God's supreme call of us both with Kathleen to His service . . . Beware lest the cares of other things, the absorption in duties, should come in.[15]

Biddy took Oswald's warning to heart and carried it with her in mothering Kathleen. Like the New Testament's Martha, she needed a reminder of where her primary responsibility lay at this busy and important time in her life. To God, yes, and to her husband, yes, but perhaps most importantly to the child God had given her—specifically Biddy Chambers—to raise.

A wise husband observes his wife in her many guises with clear eyes and love. It is a blessed woman who has such attention from her husband. In their marriage of deep love and encouragement, Oswald and Biddy never lost sight of their goals. They lived a partnership of kindred spirits.

In another letter written to the absent Biddy from a camp meeting a year later, Oswald expressed his deep feelings for his child and wife:

> Give my love to my precious little baby. I can scarcely bear to ask of her, she is so precious to my mind.
>
> I experience a great loneliness and a need of you. Not a grievous loneliness but a real loneliness. How few there are [with whom] there is any real comradeship. . . . I am quite unincorporated into anyone or anything but you and my Lord Jesus Christ. Keep praying for me.[16]

How could Biddy not adore a man whose eyes, actions, words, and prayers spoke so intimately to her? How could she not worship the God who so clearly brought them together to forge such an exciting partnership?

Askrigg saw new visitors in August 1914. Biddy and Oswald brought BTC students with them, along with Kathleen riding in a specially outfitted knapsack. They'd outgrown the Skidmores' above-the-store bedroom and rented a nearby cottage.

As Mrs. John Skidmore wrote, "There began the wonderful picnics in 'my Heavenly Father's Dining Room,' as Mr. Chambers called the moors."[17] Oswald or one of the male students packed Kathleen, fifteen months old, on his back and also carried a spirit stove (similar to a modern backpacking stove) and brewed tea and boiled potatoes to complete the picnics. Biddy and the female students joined the hikes, and a photo even exists of Miss Ashe in a prim black dress sitting on a rock, awaiting a cup of tea.

Oswald ran camp meetings, League of Prayer meetings, and open-air meetings in the villages. In the evenings, guests gathered for a weeknight service at the chapel or with the Chambers family for Bible readings. Oswald also visited friends in their homes.

Were they refreshed?

Perhaps, at the start, but within days everything changed.

On August 4, 1914, England declared war on Germany.

# 6

## The Baffling Call of God

### 1914–15

God's purpose is never man's purpose.[1]

*W*ar.

After a summer of hard-to-believe saber-rattling, the spike-helmeted German army crossed the Belgium lowlands—Flanders—with clear intentions of capturing Paris.

The Germans moved lightning-fast to catch the French by surprise following a secret plan devised in 1906 by Field Marshal Alfred von Schlieffen. No one expected Germany to invade a neutral country, much less attack Paris from the northwest.

Among the hills and dales of Yorkshire, Oswald and Biddy followed the news with a handful of BTC students. They prayed for their country, beseeching God for wisdom. They knew some students would enlist in the army and perhaps took a philosophical attitude—who better to serve than men who knew their ultimate destiny?

The first question about the source of the war came on August 5 from Charles Rae Griffin. Oswald answered him carefully:

> It is difficult to make any statements of worth in such immense moments as the present.
>
> You ask—is this dreadful war of God or the devil? I should unhesitatingly say neither of God nor the devil, but by the "patent amalgam" of both made by men and nations, James 4:1–2. . . . Men everywhere are more open to talk about God, the soul and final issues than heretofore.
>
> Don't misunderstand me, I am not inhuman, the ghastly crimes of war are unspeakable but they certainly are no worse than sin that is the crime of crimes. Jesus Our Lord says, "but when ye shall hear of wars and commotions, be not terrified," Luke 21:19. Be strong in God's love. Don't get into panics.[2]

Oswald went to the root concern: What is a person's relationship to God? Do they trust the Lord or will they choose to be fearful of events? He knew his speaking and life would be influenced by the war and the need to make sure listeners explored their faith.

Many asked Oswald about current events as he and Biddy made their rounds with the toddling Kathleen. Even in such a bucolic place far from booming artillery and marching boots, everyone worried about war. Oswald and Biddy took their concerns to the hills, where they fished, relaxed, prayed, and listened.

The Chambers family returned to a London consumed by the month-old war. Men lined up outside Scotland Yard to volunteer for the British Expeditionary Forces (BEF). Proud newly minted soldiers paraded the streets. Suffragettes momentarily set aside their militant protests and prowled Trafalgar Square urging men to enlist.

Posters of Lord Kitchener staring with a pointed finger, wanting men to join the army, blanketed the city. Patriotism ruled the day. Many expected the war to be over by Christmas with the Germans soundly beaten.

By the time the BTC began the fall term in late September, the Battle of the Marne had claimed more than five hundred thousand casualties. Armies already hunkered into trenches along both sides of Germany's western front. When Belgium's King Albert ordered his country's dikes destroyed—thus causing floods to slow the German army's advance—his nation lost all its prime agricultural land.

At #45 Clapham Common, Biddy's work remained the same: overseeing the household, welcoming students and visitors, managing the bookkeeping, keeping track of Oswald and Kathleen, and remaining calm in the face of a rapidly changing war situation.

She focused on what she could do, drawing strength from Oswald's reminder that "spiritual exhaustion never comes through sin but only through service, and whether or not you are exhausted will depend upon where you get your supplies. . . . Be exhausted for God, but remember that your supply comes from Him."[3]

The early mornings spent with the *Daily Light*, her Bible, and prayers with Oswald became even more precious. In those quiet hours Biddy prepared herself for the day with a simple prayer she used her whole life: "I give the day over into God's hands, completely, so that He will look after who comes."[4]

Cannons boomed, forests splintered, and casualties mounted in France, but Biddy had a household to look after and words to take down. She set aside her concerns to follow Jesus's lead when he found the disciples asleep: "Our Lord came to them taking the spiritual initiative against their despair and said, in effect, 'Get up, and do the next thing.' If we are inspired by God, what is the next thing? It is to trust Him absolutely."[5]

Sometimes the next thing was merely to sit down for a cup of tea with her mother.

Oswald focused on people's response to the events. To counterbalance fear, he used the most important weapon: prayer. He added thirty minutes of corporate prayer specifically for the needs of the soldiers and the nations—not just England—every morning before the usual 8:00 a.m. prayer time. He also set aside Tuesday afternoons for the entire school to pray together.

Biddy joined the prayers, no doubt relieved her forty-year-old husband's age precluded his being called up. (At the time, the BEF only enlisted men between the ages of nineteen and forty.) Oswald had never been a soldier. Indeed, through her work at the Woolwich Royal Arsenal, Biddy knew more about the military than he did.

But as they watched their nation mobilize and fight not 150 miles away across the Channel, they wondered if God might have different plans for them. Oswald could serve as a chaplain. Should this be the BTC's final year?

They prayed about the possibility.

When a donor had volunteered to endow the college years before, Oswald declined, explaining: "If you do that, it will probably go on longer than God means it to."[6] Oswald and Biddy understood the temptation to stay comfortable when God asked his people to consider altering their plans.

They decided to follow the advice about uncertainty from Habakkuk 2:3: "though it tarry, wait for it." They did not want to get ahead of God by their very desire to do his will. Oswald and Biddy were open to anything, but they waited for God's directions.

And so classes began in September 1914 with everyone on heightened alert for the future and what might happen overseas.

Home life concerned Biddy most. Kathleen was developing a mind of her own. According to Miss Ashe, Kathleen "had become a center round which the love of all the grown up men and women could be poured."[7]

She stood on her parent's chair with folded hands to say "grace" before meals. When Kathleen thought a meeting had gone on too long, she used her father's words to announce: "Shall we *wise?*" As Kathleen grew, Miss Ashe reflected on "the cordial, wonderful warmth of her smile; the trusting, confident strength of the little hand in yours; the imperious, 'go hide,' the confident 'I do it,' when she wanted you to accomplish something too hard for her baby fingers."[8]

Oswald doted on his daughter and often escorted her outside to enjoy the grassy commons or play in the small garden behind the house. In most photos where the two appear together, Oswald is focused on Kathleen, who is usually sitting on his lap, neatly dressed in startling white.

In those same photos, Biddy looks amused by her only child. Viewers can almost see her shaking her head at the two of them together.

The war did not end by Christmas 1914; rather, it already looked to be a long slog. Field Marshall Lord Kitchener expected the war to last at least three years. As the destruction deepened and casualties grew to unimaginable numbers, Oswald and Biddy recognized the profound need to offer God's consolation to soldiers, students, and families alike.

As they prayed about the upcoming new year, Oswald pointed out a verse God directed him to consider, 2 Timothy 4:6: "I am now ready to be offered." He and Biddy discussed it, and "agreed before God that it was all right as He ordained."[9] By spring 1915, Oswald concluded the time had come to make a decision. He applied to be a chaplain of the Young Men's Christian Association (YMCA).

Founded in 1844, the YMCA existed to help young men put Christian principles into practice by developing a healthy body, mind, and spirit. This goal is reflected in the three sides of a red triangle—the YMCA logo. As World War I heated up, the YMCA volunteered to handle morale and practical comforts for the Commonwealth militaries in huts stretching from Siberia to Egypt to France. These huts were manned by "secretaries" of various religious and secular occupations.

After living with Oswald's faith and his teachings for five years, Biddy had seen enough extraordinary acts of God; she could wait to see what would happen with Oswald's application. She loved her life at the BTC and may have hoped for a no from the YMCA. God knew Biddy had a toddler and no home other than #45 Clapham Common. But more than her personal happiness and security, Biddy desired God's will to prevail.

Oswald knew Proverbs 31:10–11 described his wife well: "Who can find a virtuous woman? For her price is far above rubies. The heart of her husband doth safely trust in her." And, as he wrote to his parents in May 1915:

> Biddy is just keen on the thing, and will never do anything but back me up, no matter what it costs her. Kathleen, what about her? Is it likely we would forget her or that He would? I am not several kinds of fools in one, I am only one kind of fool—the kind that believes and obeys God.[10]

Of course, Biddy supported her husband. But despite her confidence in following God's lead, sending Oswald into harm's way—even as a chaplain—meant grappling with fear. While the British government deliberately hid the truth about the slaughter on the western front, everyone mourned at least one soldier's death. Soldiers visiting the BTC routinely told stories of the muddy misery of the trenches. Pinned-up sleeves and men hobbling on crutches were common sights on the London streets eight months into the war. But Biddy handed her fears to God—especially when the YMCA accepted Oswald's application.

Ending the Bible Training College tugged at Oswald's emotions. As he wrote in his diary, "Lord, how I praise thee for this College, it has been four years of unique loveliness, and now I give it up because I believe I do so in answer to thy call."[11]

As they prepared to close the school following the spring 1915 term, Biddy organized a remembrance book for students to sign in early July. The signers reflected on what the school meant to them, as well as their affection for the Chambers family. At #45 Clapham Commons they had learned what it meant to be at God's disposal, and that their only aim was to be where God could be glorified. Several mentioned how the BTC had given them hope when they had reached the end of their own abilities.

The Bible Training College closed, "for the duration," on July 14, 1915. Oswald wrote to League of Prayer members in the August 1915 edition of *Tongues of Fire* that he expected to return to England after the war to lead another version of the BTC. Miss Ashe estimated Oswald taught more than three thousand students at the college between 1911 and 1915. More than nineteen hundred students wrote essays for the correspondence course, which also ended with the closure of the BTC. (At eight papers each, Oswald graded nearly sixteen thousand essays, stamped them with his red signature, and returned them to the faithful Gertrude to mail.)

August 1915 saw Biddy, Kathleen, and Oswald, along with BTC students and Oswald's siblings Arthur, Gertrude, and Bertha, in Askrigg for one last holiday. Oswald spoke on the psalms of ascent, Psalms 120–34, during the evening hour in their small cottage and in local chapels. Every evening ended with a special prayer for the men serving on the front lines.

By then they knew Oswald would leave for Egypt in the fall. The YMCA had assigned Oswald to serve in a YMCA hut, most likely in a desert camp—the majority were located not far from Alexandria (on the Mediterranean), Port Said (at the northern entrance to the Suez Canal), or Cairo (inland on the Nile).

The British Army had not yet declared Egypt a closed military zone in 1915. Australian and New Zealand Army Corps (ANZAC) soldiers had invaded Gallipoli, 650 miles across the Mediterranean Sea from Alexandria, but actual fighting had not yet come to Egypt. While skirmishes occurred in the Sinai Desert and in the west toward Libya, Egypt—a protectorate of England—remained a training and staging area at the time.

Military hospitals, only then starting to receive patients from the Gallipoli campaign, were located primarily in Alexandria and Cairo.

William Jessop, the Anglo-American head of the International YMCA in Egypt and the Middle East, lived with his wife in a Cairo apartment. The couple was childless; in fact, none of the twelve secretaries in theater on June 30, 1915, brought wives or children to Egypt. Certainly missionaries with children lived there, but they were longtime residents and not YMCA-affiliated.

James 4:2 said "ye have not, because ye ask not," so Oswald prayed and then made an impossible request to the small YMCA staff in Egypt: since Egypt wasn't a war zone like France, could he bring his family?

Who would think to ask such a question but a man tuned to God's lead?

Some civilians, including women and children, still traveled to Egypt. Was Biddy willing to take a toddler to a hot, insect-ridden desert filled with soldiers and the likelihood of illness?

Yes, and loyal Mary Riley volunteered to come with her.

Given Oswald's reminder that Kathleen was their gift to cherish from God, they never considered leaving her behind. (At that time, missionaries and military families overseas kept young ones with them and sent school-aged children to boarding schools in their home countries.)

Dais still worked her busy job five and a half days a week, and Emily couldn't manage the gregarious Kathleen in a boarding house. Biddy's brother, Bert, and his wife, Beatrice, had their own child, Jack, who was the same age as Kathleen, but they were not interested in the things of God and so wouldn't make acceptable guardians for Kathleen.

Oswald's brothers had their own lives and children; his sisters were not married. Gertrude had her hands full with her parents. And so they could not leave Kathleen with family even if they wanted to.

The impossible happened. The YMCA gave permission for Biddy and Kathleen to join Oswald in Egypt—at their own expense. And Miss Riley could come as Kathleen's nurse.

Tempting though it might have been to travel together—Oswald was due to sail on October 9—Biddy and Oswald made the prudent decision to send him ahead to examine the situation and prepare a place for the family. They didn't have the funds in hand for the family to travel at the moment, anyway.

Once Oswald's orders became known, two BTC alumni also joined the YMCA for service in Egypt: Jimmy Hanson and Philip Hancock. Others planned to apply: Miss Ashe, Gladys Ingram, Kathleen Ballinger, and Eva Spink. Oswald referred to the group as "the BTC Expeditionary Force."

Following their Askrigg holiday, Biddy and Kathleen returned to #45 Clapham Common with Mary Riley. Oswald remained behind in Yorkshire during September to work with local soldiers.

He traveled to London in early October to pack, write letters, and make arrangements for his possessions. Some he left behind in stored trunks but others he gave away. Oswald presented Eva with the Bible he had used and written his notes in for the last seven years. It became a prized possession.

Oswald also purchased items necessary for Egypt, including his YMCA uniform.

The YMCA designed their uniform for secretaries (they were all male) after a British officer's khaki-colored uniform. Oswald wore a "peaked" hat with a bill that came to a triangle above his forehead, with an insignia under the peak. He tucked his shirt and tie into a lapelled tunic with four buttons down the front and epaulets on the shoulders. Two breast pockets above and two large pockets big enough for books or maps under the belt line covered the front of the uniform. Trousers from the same woolen material reached to his shiny black shoes.

In keeping with Egyptian weather, he also could wear a pith helmet—a brimmed hat that looked like a canvas soup bowl turned upside down. It kept off the sun's heat and could be worn with a cloth extending over the back of his neck for sunburn protection.

Like most men, Oswald looked dapper in uniform.

He packed books, plenty of writing materials, and the prayers of many. Biddy knew he went by God's direction, but the sea was dangerous in 1915.

German *Unterseeboots* (U-boats) cruised under the waters off the coast of England and France and throughout the Mediterranean Sea. Ships were torpedoed regularly and Oswald was to travel on a BEF troop transport ship, a prized target for the navies of the Central Powers (Germany, Austria-Hungry, and Turkey). A U-boat had sunk the RMS *Lusitania* off the Irish coast only a few months before.

Biddy tried to keep her upper lip stiff but couldn't control her tears on October 9, 1915. They prayed together, again and again, until Oswald felt he could leave.

And then he walked out the door.

Biddy dealt with the anguish of his departure by focusing on the next thing and getting on with her duties. When a knock came several hours later, she discovered a grinning Oswald on the doorstep. Departure had been delayed twenty-four hours.

Military wives will tell you having your husband return once you've started to make your peace with his departure makes it harder to let him go a second time.

After Oswald departed the next day, Biddy read the letter he left for her and undoubtedly wept again:

> You are bearing these days well. When you married me, I had no prospects, but just Him, and you had just me, and you loved me with a love that has been a shield and joy and a rampart of strength to me. Now God has given us our darling Kathleen and we go forth again.
>
> You have loved this place. It has been Bethel to you, a great joyous place and God's benediction. . . .

I go forth without College and without students and without
a calling, just to speak and be for Him, and you will go with me.
Our years together have been radiantly blessed and now the few
weeks apart will be radiant with His perfections.[12]

Shortly after Oswald's departure, Biddy received letters recount-
ing his days at sea aboard the SS *City of Paris*. He described a full
ship and how he took refuge in a lifeboat for time alone with God.
Of greatest interest to her personally was the letter written two
days after his departure:

I have scarcely missed you, so completely and entirely have you been
with me. The sense of God's presence is real and beautiful. The
sense also is so entire that my going is of Him and His ways that
although I cannot begin to discern what I am to do out in Egypt,
I am not even concerned.[13]

While he knew his wife was entirely capable of anything, Oswald asked Gladys Ingram to help Biddy prepare for the trip to
Egypt. He also wrote Eva's skeptical parents, thanking them for
her support and aid to his wife and child.

Gladys and Eva moved home as they awaited news about their
own prospects for going to Egypt. They didn't live far away—
Gladys in Wimbledon and Eva at her family's estate at Chisle-
hurst, Kent. Their love for the Chambers family, coupled with
their own interest, often brought them to visit at #45 Clapham
Common.

They rejoiced with Biddy when she received a wire announcing
Oswald's safe arrival in Port Said, Egypt, on October 26, 1915.
He met his boss, William Jessop, at the pier and they caught
the "milk and honey express" train to Cairo, arriving by late
afternoon.

Jessop and his wife, Mary, introduced the new secretary to such
a crowd of people at their apartment the first night that Oswald
didn't get to bed until midnight.

The next morning, Oswald attended a conference of YMCA sec-retaries that helped him better understand the situation in Egypt. As he wrote in his diary:

> I listened and wondered how God was going to engineer circum-stances for Biddy to come and work with me here, but we shall see. God always performs wonders.[14]

# 7

## The Undetected Sacredness of Circumstances

### 1915

The circumstances of a saint's life are ordained of God.[1]

*N*o longer a Bible training college, #45 Clapham Common echoed without Oswald and the students. Mrs. Howard Hooker visited often, along with other members of the League of Prayer, as they tried to determine the next steps with the house.

Biddy helped tie up the ends of closing the college as needed. She also prepared for the major change liable to come at any moment. Letters took one to three weeks to travel between Egypt and London—assuming they didn't go awry, which was always a possibility when the mail traveled by U-boat–vulnerable ship. Biddy expected to receive a telegram from Oswald one day simply telling her to come.

While the YMCA paid secretaries a yearly stipend of forty pounds (US $4000, 2014) plus travel monies and housing, none of those funds arrived before Oswald sailed. Biddy's expenses would have to be covered from her own pocket or, more likely, from God's providence. While she awaited Oswald's directions, she made plans for life in Egypt.

Biddy could glean information from a popular guide book of the day, Karl Baedeker's detailed 1915 *Egypt and the Sudan*.[2] Baedeker's guide provided details such as the names of physicians in Cairo, the cost to ride the trams, and drawings of Egyptian money, the *piastre*. It also included railway guides and maps for tourist and historic locations. Small enough to be easily carried, *Egypt and the Sudan* described both past and contemporary Egyptian life and warned never to eat salad or unpeeled vegetables. The book even included a basic Egyptian vocabulary with pronunciation instructions.

As Biddy made lists, she paid close attention to Baedeker's clothing suggestions:

> For all ordinary purposes a couple of light tweed suits, a few flannel and soft cotton shirts, a supply of thin woolen socks, one pair of light and easy boots, one of shoes, and one of slippers, a moderately warm cloak, a pith helmet and a soft felt hat or a straw hat, together with the most necessary articles of the toilet will suffice. . . . All articles should be new and strongly made, as it is often difficult to get repairs properly executed in Egypt.[3]

She bought a pith helmet and the necessary clothing for herself and Kathleen. She turned all British correspondence responsibilities over to Gertrude to forward the mail, and spent as much time as possible with her mother and sister. Once organized, Biddy waited and prayed while Oswald mused in his diary about whether she missed him as much as he missed her.

Of course she did.

But the situation in Egypt was complicated.

When the YMCA's international committee asked William Jessop to move from Calcutta to Cairo in 1913 and take over the fledgling branch, they provided only a tiny budget. As Jessop described the unsavory population of 650,000, "the moral tone of Cairo, or the lack of it, is notorious."[4] He was still piecing together a ministry with foreign donations when war broke out in 1914.

In his 1922 book, *Service with Fighting Men: An Account of the Work of the American Young Men's Christian Associations in the World War*, former US president William H. Taft recounted Egypt's effects on ANZAC soldiers arriving there in early 1915. He noted the majority of the men were Australians or New Zealanders, "vigorous, undisciplined men of the frontier," encountering brothels and the decadence of a cosmopolitan city for the first time, and "the venereal problem developed at an alarming rate."[5]

The situation was, indeed, complicated.

By the summer of 1915, one hundred thousand troops were stationed in and around Cairo—the British Expeditionary Forces (BEF) perched on Mokattam Hill in the Citadel, the Australians camped near the pyramids, and the New Zealanders drilled north at Zeitoun. The Red Cross transformed Mena Hotel, a former hunting lodge within sight of the pyramids, into a hospital.

Military authorities welcomed the work of the YMCA and other ministries, if only to keep their men healthy. Jessop and his staff accepted the challenge. Soldiers had little to do at the camps while off duty and limited opportunities to visit town when granted passes. Once in Cairo, they flocked to houses of ill repute, and hundreds contracted venereal diseases. Port Said, at the north end of the Suez Canal, housed the largest red-light district in the world.

Shortly before Oswald's arrival, the YMCA leased three acres of central Cairo's Ezbekieh Park just down the street from Shepheard's Hotel, where British and army officials billeted. Located near the notorious "Fish Market" area of ill repute, the Ezbekieh Gardens YMCA ministry averaged sixteen hundred soldier visitors a day.

Volunteers helped YMCA secretaries run an open-air theater that could seat up to three thousand at a time. English women served tea and ran a restaurant; by the final year of the war, American donations to the YMCA funded an outdoor swimming pool. Soldiers mailed thousands of letters from Ezbekieh every day, and the men could hear concerts, see movies, play billiards and other games, roller-skate, and attend lectures.

British generals loved the work of the YMCA because it kept the men busy with more wholesome activities than those provided by local brothels.[6] Before the development of penicillin in 1952, venereal disease could be a death sentence, and the army's harsh treatment of the disease—both medically and administratively—sobered many soldiers, along with fears of taking it home to their loved ones at war's end.

After the incessant drills in the desert heat, battling flies as well as anticipated enemies, many soldiers visited the YMCA "huts" located either near or in their army camps, seeking resources, encouragement, and refreshments. In the first six months of the war, secretaries at the handful of YMCA locations in Egypt provided over a million sheets of correspondence paper to soldiers writing home.[7]

During Oswald's first days in Egypt, Jessop toured him around Cairo and then took him out to his station at Zeitoun. Oswald liked the location immediately, remarking: "This is absolutely desert in the very heart of the troops and a glorious opportunity for men. It is all immensely unlike anything I have been used to, and I am watching with interest the new things God will do and engineer."[8]

Located seven miles north of Cairo, a mere electric tram ride from Ezbekieh Gardens downtown, the YMCA hut at Zeitoun—actually a large marquee tent resembling a circus big top—sat on grounds belonging to the Egyptian General Mission (EGM). Encircled by a waist-high stone wall, the EGM compound at Zeitoun included a square, white, two-story building housing the large family of EGM secretary George Swan. A sprawling ANZAC encampment surrounded three sides of the compound, with the eastern end facing empty desert.

The EGM was founded by a group of English and Irish men in 1897, loosely linked to and inspired by the Holiness Movement. In seven sites stretching from Cairo to the Nile delta and over to Ismailia on the Suez Canal, the missionary group oversaw schools and a hospital. They also ran a book depot selling Christian books and other materials produced by EGM-sponsored Nile Mission Press. The EGM worked closely with the YMCA in all their locations throughout the war, and George Swan welcomed the new chaplain to Zeitoun. It's plausible the EGM missionaries had even heard of Oswald Chambers before he arrived.

Oswald would conduct his daily activities within the canvas hut, which included a small office for him. With a raised platform at one end featuring the requisite British flag and a pump organ, the hut provided sufficient tables and folding chairs for up to three hundred men at a time. Users were the ANZAC soldiers who served with the infantry, field artillery brigade, and the mounted rifles—which meant horses (and thus flies) in the camp. Troops were training for the Gallipoli quagmire and the anticipated Sinai Peninsula invasion.

The only women in sight, besides Mrs. Dora Swan of the EGM, were native workers performing menial chores such as cooking and laundry.

As Oswald walked through his new responsibilities, he noticed signs posted by his predecessor, Mr. Oatts: "Please remember you are in a YMCA hut and don't use bad language." "A short prayer meeting will be held in the Secretary's cubicle each evening at 8:45." "Bring back that pen."[9]

Oswald immediately removed the notices. As Theodore At-kinson, a London opera singer turned corporal, wrote about the new secretary: "It was never necessary to ask the men not to swear when Mr. Chambers was about."[10]

His first night in charge, Oswald mounted the platform at the front of the tent and announced prayer time would be at 8:45—he wanted to give those men not interested time to leave. Atkinson noted the new secretary's voice "rang through the spiritually dead atmosphere of our hut," and everyone left.[11]

Oswald held the prayer time anyway, and the following night several soldiers joined him.

An enormous change began to sweep through the huts as Oswald cheerfully moved among the soldiers. Within weeks, a number of men were staying for prayer and participating in an hour-long Bible study. Oswald cancelled entertainments in the evening and provided, instead, straight teaching from the Word of God.

The only sign he posted was a banner proclaiming Luke 11:13 across the wall behind the raised platform from which he addressed the men: "If ye, then, being evil, know how to give good gifts unto your children; how much more shall your heavenly Father give the Holy Spirit to them that ask him?" His personal ministry tools soon included a blackboard for outline talks and a large table stocked with League of Prayer literature.

The Citadel YMCA secretary, Reverend Douglas Downes, journeyed to Zeitoun one evening and "found the unheard of thing had come to pass. Men whom no one could accuse of being religious, turned up in large numbers on a week-night to hear a religious talk."[12] One of the soldiers Downes met reported his life as being completely transformed by Oswald's teaching.

Outside the compound walls, desert stretched east as far as the eye could see. The fine, dusty sand drifted through the air and settled on everything. The heat beat down and flies swarmed in hordes. Oswald immediately obtained a fly whisk—something like a large artist's paintbrush with long bristles—to scatter the incessant pests. (As one recent visitor to Egypt noted, "You get used to having twenty or so flies on you at any time."[13])

At night, the noisy army camp lit the western view with electric light. A thin glow from the south indicated Cairo proper. Several miles north, a businessman ran a brightly lit amusement center at Heliopolis. To the east, white stars prickled a black night stretching over the desert to dip behind distant hills.

Oswald looked to the east. Just as he loved the limitless ocean on his sea voyages, Oswald appreciated the desert's vast emptiness and changing colors. He liked to wrap himself in an army-issued blanket and sit outside his tent, eating his rations and watching the sunrise in its infinite glory.

Meanwhile, in England, Biddy waited for word she could join him, often consulting with Charles Griffin. Griffin had assumed responsibility for the Chambers' publishing-related ventures with Oswald's departure. When the BTC closed, he arranged to use any profit on the Discipline booklet series for BTC-type work in Egypt. Because they were fond of the Chambers family, Griffin and his wife, Norah, volunteered to pay for Biddy, Kathleen, and Mary Riley's passage to Egypt.

Oswald finally wired for them to come on November 17. He received a "word" from God in his morning study from Mark 9:8 ("Suddenly, when they had looked round about, they saw no man any more, save Jesus only with themselves") and Psalm 37:4 ("Delight thyself also in the LORD: and he shall give thee the desires of thine heart").

It was time for Biddy to purchase tickets.

Jubilant to soon be reunited with his family, Oswald wrote a friend: "I scarcely know what to do for joy at the prospect of having her [Biddy] again. I love her more than any love can state."[14]

But where would they live?

The EGM's George Swan offered a spot in the compound to build a small bungalow. They drew a plan in the sand—basically a long, narrow rectangle—and Oswald made arrangements. With the army camp on three sides, the compound fell within the security zone monitored by military guards, and thus it would be convenient for the Chambers family with their "ministry of interruptions" to open their house to all who sought God's help.

Oswald possessed no funds to build but expected God to supply what he required. God confirmed the decision when Oswald read the *Daily Light* verse that night, taken from 2 Chronicles 6:18: "Behold, heaven and the heaven of heavens cannot contain thee; how much less this house which I have built!"

The intrepid Griffin began raising money. Worshipers at Speke Hall ultimately donated £88 (US $6000, 2014)[15] to build and outfit the Zeitoun bungalow.

Oswald found native workers to make the same clay, silt, straw, and sand bricks the Israelites had made during Moses's time. Generally ten by fourteen inches in size, these inexpensive and easy to build mud bricks enabled quick construction. Their time-proven insulation factor permitted the bungalow to retain heat in the relatively cooler winter months and provide shelter from the sweltering summer sun.

Barely two weeks later, Oswald walked through the bungalow to dedicate it to God for His purposes, just as he and Biddy had done at the BTC. The simple Egyptian bungalow was a far cry from the Cedar Terrace townhouse, but Oswald knew God could use it to his glory.

Biddy purchased tickets on a Bibby Line steamship, the SS *Herefordshire*, which sailed between Liverpool and Rangoon to provision and transport British nationals, along with carrying the mail. They embarked December 10 out of Liverpool.

Eva sent Oswald a wire as soon as the ship sailed.

They traveled in a first-class compartment like everyone else on board, apprehensive at the dangers lurking under the restless Atlantic. Thirty-two-year-old Biddy calmed her fears by remembering her love for the sea, praying, and reading Scripture. Thirty-five-year-old Miss Riley had never sailed before but was determined to help Biddy with Kathleen, the sole child among the twenty-five passengers. The Chambers party of three and a glamorous American couple on a special trade permit from the US government would be the only travelers disembarking at Port Said.

As they sailed the first day, Biddy opened the first note Oswald had sent for the voyage. She had thirteen—one for each day of the trip. It had been his habit to leave a note on her pillow whenever he traveled overnight; now he provided for her voyage. He had written and sent them from Egypt as soon as Biddy confirmed her travel plans.

Biddy might not have Oswald's human presence with her on the ship, but she held his loving and thoughtful words in her hands.

Always.

In typical Oswald fashion, the short notes spoke of his love for her and Kathleen and his faith in God, and also made a few references to her location: "How do you like the Mediterranean?" She read many such simple statements over the next two weeks.

"And I'll give you rest and a lovely day."

"Sleep blessedly my own darling wife."

"Kiss Kathleen."

"How wonderfully God arranges each detail."

At the end of each note he signed himself, "your loving husband, Oswald."[16]

As a penniless, traveling teacher, Oswald Chambers had not expected God to give him a wife, but once he married Biddy he cherished her. While he appreciated Biddy as a partner, poetry-loving Oswald did not miss an opportunity to shower her with romantic endearments.

He trusted God implicitly, but Oswald knew she risked her life and that of their child to travel over dangerous waters during a war. On the other hand, he knew how much his wife enjoyed a voyage and laughed in a letter to Gladys Ingram about how her soul must be glowing to be at sea again.

Maybe, but Biddy had never sailed in the winter before.

The *Herefordshire* steamed out of Liverpool across the rough Irish Sea, through St. George's Channel, and into the frigid Atlantic Ocean off England's southwestern tip. The crew advised passengers to scan the water's surface on the off chance they might see a submarine's periscope. The ship sailed in a zigzag course to confuse possible tracking U-boats, but they would not know they'd crossed paths with one until they saw a torpedo plume on the surface—or were struck.

The crew issued life jackets to the passengers, including Kathleen, with orders to keep them close at all times. Tension grew the first day out when they got news that a British cargo ship, the SS *Pinegrove*, had struck a mine and sank in the English Channel eight miles west of Calais.

As the weather that December consisted of driving winds and high seas, seasickness plagued passengers and the majority stayed indoors rather than risk strolling on the heaving deck. Sea water pounded the ship and rain poured off every surface as they journeyed along the coasts of France, Portugal, and Spain. In spite of it, Biddy may very well have prayed a thanksgiving prayer: foul weather decreased the likelihood U-boats would find them, much less launch a torpedo.

The *Herefordshire* sailed at night through the blacked-out Straits of Gibraltar to elude any U-boats lurking near the bottleneck into the Mediterranean Sea. Searchlights from British-controlled Gibraltar were the only visible signs of activity on the dark shores. Winter rain fell in even the protected Mediterranean, and seasickness left the passengers moaning in their bunks.

Given the chanciness of sailing schedules, Oswald did not know the exact date of their arrival—which was why one of his final messages advised Biddy to find an official traveler's aide to help offload her luggage when they arrived in Port Said. Oswald's December 22 diary entry praised God about her anticipated arrival, noting British officials had changed their policies for Egypt that very week and no more civilian women would be allowed into the country.

Reasons to praise God became more evident when the *Herefordshire* neared Port Said. Biddy watched from the starboard deck as they passed the remains of a Japanese steamer, the *Macceim*, and an old tanker recently sunk by U-boat torpedoes.[17]

The *Herefordshire* reached the statue of Suez Canal architect Ferdinand de Lesseps early on December 27 and docked at Port Said—where a beaming Oswald waited at the pier. Describing the ache he felt at missing his wife as nearly "unto death," he hugged and kissed her with great relief. Biddy marveled to see her thin husband again, looking like a soldier in his neatly pressed khaki clothing with his face sunburned to a mahogany brown. Oswald picked up his daughter, greeted Miss Riley, arranged for the baggage, and escorted them to the train station for a five-hour express train ride to Cairo.

Rattling down the western bank of the Suez Canal toward Ismailia, Biddy, Kathleen, and Mary Riley blinked their eyes at the change in scenery. The silky waters of the blue canal presented a contrast to the scrappy desert hovels to the west. Ninety minutes south, the town of Ismailia rose like an oasis of faded greenery muggy with heat before the train turned west to cross the biblical Goshen lands.

Every window afforded a new sight: trudging buffalo harnessed to waterwheels drawing water from wells, white conical pigeon houses bristling with stick perches, sinewy farmers cultivating vegetable fields, mandarin orange groves giving way to vineyards. At Benha the train joined the main tracks and chugged another hour south to Cairo.

As they neared Cairo's Misr—the train station on the north end of the sprawling, block-like city—Biddy looked across the life-giving Nile to three pyramids and a sphinx silhouetted against the sunset on the Giza plain. Woolwich, Askrigg, and Clapham Common all seemed very far away.

Fortunately, Mrs. Chambers enjoyed a little adventure now and then.

They stepped into an exotic station that was crowded and noisy with the colonial twang of brawny soldiers and the musical babble of white-robed porters. Burly men in white togas wore cylindrical felt caps with golden tassels swinging to the beat of their footsteps. The heavy smells, moist air, and genuine surprise left Biddy and Mary wide-eyed until William and Mary Jessop stepped forward to welcome them.

The Jessops loaned their Cairo apartment to the Chambers party for their first two days in Egypt. Oswald soon introduced them to the sights and sounds of the foreign city: Kahn el Kalili market's spicy scents, Ezbekieh Gardens' tropical greenery, Shepheard's Hotel's tea parlor, and Groppi's famous French pastries and ice cream.

Under the British occupation, street signs originally written in Arabic now included a French and English translation. They rode Egyptian *gharries*—horse-drawn buggies—through the streets and marveled at the sights. Minarets spun to the sky at the citadel that towered over the city, hookah smoke blew from cramped doorways, and local women mingled with upper class British women escorted by uniformed menfolk. Soldiers roamed everywhere.

With Biddy's arrival, followed a few days later by Jimmy Hanson and Philip Hancock, the first wave of the "BTC Expeditionary Force" had arrived in Egypt.

The weather was difficult, the war imminent, the men desperate. God had moved all the principals unexpectedly into place; it was time for the ministry to begin.

Biddy and Oswald were ready.

# 8

## The Determination to Serve

### *1916*

Nothing . . . can exhaust our determination to serve men for His sake.[1]

*T*he Chambers party caught the electric tram near the Jessop home and rode it north through the dirty, cramped streets of sprawling Cairo in the waning days of 1915. The tram's ultimate destination was Heliopolis, but they got off at the penultimate stop, Helmieh Station, disembarking with their baggage in front of a line of native businesses separated from the tracks by a rickety white fence.

Brisk military men took their places and the tram trundled away. Dark-skinned fortune-tellers crouched along the fence, smoothing the sand and calling to passersby in a singsong language. A small woman swathed in black veils strolled by with an enormous square basket on her head. Charcoal braziers spiced the air as "Tommies"—British soldiers—gathered to dicker over prices.

Oswald found men to haul their trunks the mile to their new home and they set off on foot. Oswald carried Kathleen and Biddy trudged through the soft sand, thankful for Baedeker's recommended sturdy boots. She and Miss Riley wrinkled their noses at the pungent smell of horses, smoke, and latrines.

To the northeast, rows of white, bell-shaped tents marked the ANZAC encampment. The activity and noise astounded: pounding horses, loping camels, shouting infantrymen, and screaming artillery. Distant, dusty clouds indicated maneuvers. Drifts of silty, thick air spread over them.

Biddy adjusted her pith helmet against the bright winter sun.

They walked through the middle of the camp, past a post office, supply depot, and a series of white, colonial-style buildings, including the two-story regimental headquarters and a motor pool. They turned south at the mineral water factory and followed a footpath skirting a variety of outbuildings, tents, and groups of laboring orderlies. Dateless stone pillars lay in broken clumps, as Biddy already had observed out the train window. Ancient civilizations brushed up against modern life all over Egypt.

Oswald indicated a rock-walled area with a large square sign proclaiming "YMCA" in blue letters inside a red triangle. When they reached the eastern entrance, Biddy saw what looked like a circus tent on the southern side of the compound and a two-story whitewashed building outside the north wall. "The EGM home of the Swans," Oswald explained. Drooping trees bent toward the house, while inside the rock walls of the compound the empty brown sand lay barren.

Except when a cloud of flies rose to light elsewhere.

"Absolute desert," she murmured, remembering Oswald's description.

He touched her elbow and pointed to a mud-brown structure forty feet west of the tent.

Home.

It was hard to imagine a place less like #45 Clapham Common.

She stepped through the wide opening in the wall and walked past the tent toward the "bungalow" for a closer inspection.

A simple roof made of thick native matting covered the long, narrow building. Four window openings and two doorways faced east, away from the army hubbub outside the wall. Biddy and Oswald and perhaps Kathleen took one small room, and Miss Riley moved into the other.

Furnishings were basic: rustic beds, wall hooks for clothing, and their trunks. Several canvas camping chairs, with their wooden feet dug into the sand for anchoring, provided seating whether indoors or out. Mosquito nets lay across each bed, with a hook in the ceiling above from which to hang them. The rest of daily life took place outside.

Compared to this, Askrigg's "heavenly dining room" was a banquet hall.

Biddy straightened her shoulders and bestowed a gentle smile on her watching husband. Where they lived didn't matter; they were together again. They prayed in both rooms, consecrating the bungalow and the compound to God's work.

As Oswald wrote in his diary: "God be praised. Here I am all after the desire of my heart, in the center of a great military encampment and Biddy and Kathleen and Miss Riley here with me. Hallelujah!"[2]

The Swan family with its five children—Barbara, Martin, Douglas, John David, and baby Hugh Christopher—swarmed to greet them. Kathleen and David, nearly the same age, soon became inseparable. Biddy and Dora Swan also became fast friends.

Biddy rolled up the cotton sleeves of her white shirtwaist, straightened the pith helmet on her head, and stepped up to the task of turning the bungalow into suitable living quarters. Within the walls of that basic shelter, Biddy made their home.

The soldiers immediately noticed the presence of two women and a toddling girl in the camp. Theo Atkinson, the opera singer turned soldier, appreciated the changes Oswald brought to the YMCA hut but marked his family's arrival as a turning point: "Things got better and better. They kept open house for us all. Whatever they had they shared, and with little Kathleen running around and attending the Sunday services where she lustily sang the hymns, and Miss Riley's cooking, we began to feel almost as if we were home again."[3]

Biddy wanted to be where God placed her to work with Oswald. It would be a challenge to tend Kathleen in a land of dirt, sand, insects, heat, and thirst, but plenty of well-meaning people wanted to help. Most importantly, God remained her refuge and her strength, a very present help in trouble. She did not fear; God would help her.

As would the servants. No one expected a woman straight from England to manage the hard labor of desert housekeeping. Miss Riley and an army orderly assigned to help the YMCA soon mastered cooking over the cookstove. Egyptian locals came to the bungalow to handle the laundry—a complicated task with their light-colored clothing. Biddy laughed as she watched the laundresses fill their mouths with water and spit onto the clean clothes to dampen them for ironing.[4]

Oswald's uniform always looked immaculate, even in the diabolical heat of summer. As for Biddy, she dressed in light, layered clothing, arms and legs covered to keep off the sun but also because she felt cooler wearing loose clothes (being hot and moist under long sleeves felt more comfortable than being hot and dry under the sun).[5] Photos of Kathleen show a plucky little girl in white knee-length dresses, white socks, Mary Jane shoes, and a large bow in her hair.

There were advantages to owning only a few garments and little furniture—the morning housework didn't take long. After she made the beds, Biddy only had to smooth the sandy floor each morning. Housekeeping done!

One soldier wrote admiringly of the "women who labored with him [Oswald] in the gospel in conditions at times heart-breaking, self-relegated, all because of their conviction that he was in the will of God."⁶ Tommies recognized the price Biddy and the others paid to serve God in Egypt.

Two British women and a little girl drew those men like honey. Soldiers soon begged Biddy to let them help during their off-duty hours. Geoffrey Cumine assisted Biddy with local shopping and won Kathleen's affections immediately. Australian Ted Strach dug a garden and planted bushes and flowers under Biddy's direction. He gathered stones to outline paths between the huts and toiled in the hot sun to finish the project before his unit shipped out to France.

Ten days after arriving at Zeitoun, Biddy sat in a canvas camping chair gloating over a fat packet of mail from England. As she wrote Eva Spink on January 10, 1916: "I sat outside the hut with the most beautiful sunrise radiating everywhere and just had a perfectly lovely time reading. . . . It's an ideal day again, cloudless sun and a blue sky with a lovely cool air underneath as it were."⁷

Her chatty letter touched on spiritual matters concerning Eva, as well as comments about clothing. Washing Kathleen's hair in the dry climate was easy; she had met an interesting American woman on the ship. "We continually talk of you and Gladiolus [Gladys Ingram] when we are in town and what it would be like to have you around with us."⁸

The Spink family did not want their determined daughter to travel to Egypt during a war to work in a YMCA camp.⁹ Biddy praised Eva's resolution: "I'm so glad you told us about your talk with your father as for your being absolutely and adamantly His [God's]. He will make your path plain." Biddy also touched on the challenges of mothering a precocious two-and-a-half-year-old: "I'm still learning much from watching Kathleen. She seems a picture of human nature which needs to be rightly adjusted. She is a benediction from heaven." Biddy delighted in watching her daughter play with the Swan children and the doting soldiers.¹⁰

Kathleen's favorite playmates included a British peer, the Right Honorable Lord Radstock, senior YMCA leader in Egypt. A bachelor in his fifties, he and Kathleen doted on each other. She liked to dress up her dolls as uniformed soldiers, and when "Lord Rad" visited, she'd make him get down on his hands and knees to pray for the dolls. She even asked him to baptize the dolls one day. Lord Rad always obliged.

She had pets too: Geoffrey Cumine gave her a kitten; other soldiers brought her rabbits (which did not live long) and a dog.

Kathleen's behavior served an important role in the camp, as one admirer recounted: "The ring and echo of her laughter has sounded in many an ear like a joyful sound long forgotten . . . when the children of their hearts and of every day were around them."[11]

Jimmy Hanson also fell in with Kathleen, and she shared her candy with him whenever she received two pieces.

Jimmy and Philip Hancock stayed at Zeitoun their first months in Egypt, but eventually William Jessop assigned them other tasks. YMCA demands were so pressing that Jessop couldn't leave three able-bodied secretaries in one place. He assigned Jimmy to a nearby hut so Oswald could oversee his work and periodically teach a class there. Philip billeted with troops on the Suez Canal. They both visited Zeitoun whenever the opportunity arose or they craved a taste of home.

In February, Oswald received word that Miss Katherine Ashe had somehow convinced the YMCA to sponsor her into Egypt. Leaving Kathleen behind in Miss Riley's care, Oswald and Biddy traveled to Port Said to meet the ship, but British authorities refused to admit the fifty-year-old woman. They detained Miss Ashe with the intention of shipping her home on the next boat headed to England.

Oswald and Biddy spent the night in Port Said and took a walk along the breakwater to pray. That night Oswald wrote in his diary:

The young moon was clear and beautiful, the sea breaking in long sweeping rolls, and the night sky the wonderful purple of the East . . . as we remained silent for a while there came to us distinctly the words, "It is I, be not afraid," and we stood still in awe. It would not have been at all surprising had we seen Him coming to us on the water.[12]

They returned to Cairo the next day with no expectation they would be able to see Miss Ashe. By the time their train arrived at the Misr station, however, the British authorities had changed their minds and permitted Miss Ashe entry into the country. Oswald and Biddy laughed at God's often unexpected ways.

Her severe black dress, snowy hair, and thin figure looked completely out of place in the sandy compound. Miss Ashe later described Zeitoun in typically poetic terms:

A space of sand within a low stone wall set in the open desert with, for interpreters, the desert sky, and the desert's limitless space. . . . The house faced eastwards and looked clear out towards the morning, to the peace and to coming life of the world.[13]

She stayed at Zeitoun for the first month, adjusting to the climate, before Jessop sent her to the Soldier's Home in Alexandria. Overseen by Lady Godley, the staff included a nursing sister and orderlies. Built to house the sultan's bodyguard, the rest home nestled amid a big garden near the sea, and in 1916 it housed recovering veterans of the Gallipoli disaster.[14]

Biddy quickly set up a schedule at Zeitoun. She and Oswald still rose early in the morning to read the *Daily Light*, study the Bible, pray, and discuss the day. They loved the glorious sunrises and both filled letters home describing the enormous sky from sunrise to sunset.

The household met for prayers at 7:15 each morning and then ate breakfast. Afterward, everyone went to their duties—cooking, cleaning, organizing, letter writing, tending Kathleen, or whatever else turned up. Biddy and Mary Riley served a meal at noon, and then everyone took a three-hour rest in the hot afternoon. The compound was hushed, "utterly silent—as each one spent the resting space as he or she desired. Silence reigned without also—for the midday 'rest' was a rule in Camp as well—and native servants in Egypt always sleep during the heat of the day," Miss Ashe explained.[15] The only exception was Oswald, who spent the afternoon trekking through the scorching sun to visit soldiers in military hospitals.

The women prepared a simple tea at 3:00, when visitors tended to arrive from Cairo or neighboring camps. Adept at stretching food, Biddy and Miss Riley never worried about an extra guest or even a dozen at supper. They also served an informal meal—mostly sandwiches and fruit—at 6:30.

Tommies trooped in when their day finished around 6:00 and thronged the huts until closing time at 10:00. Just before 7:30, Biddy would pick up her pencil and notebook and follow Oswald to his lecture. She attended every night to take down everything he said. In many ways, her life continued just as it had at the BTC, only in different weather and more complicated circumstances.

The focus of the ministry was also different. Whereas at the BTC Oswald had prepared missionaries for the field, in Zeitoun he and Biddy lived as missionaries.

The majority of soldiers who visited the marquee tent were destined for warfare either on the Sinai Peninsula (marching to Jerusalem) or in France. Some had survived Gallipoli's horrors and expected to see more—they all knew about the misery of trench warfare. With spiritual destinies balanced between the past and the future, Oswald and Biddy, along with the others attached to the EGM and the YMCA, sought to present the gospel in a way the soldiers could grasp.

As a result, Oswald gave (and Biddy took down) teachings on "His Cost and Our Discipleship" and, in mid-February, an entire series on "The Sermon on the Mount." Students included soldiers from all walks of life and, as Oswald wrote, "they shove in crowding round afterwards with their questions and eager thirst for Bible knowledge [that] exceeds anything I have ever known."[16]

Oswald always conversed with soldiers until the tent closed, just before the army camp's 10:15 curfew. Many nights after the men departed, Oswald and Biddy walked across the cooling desert sands to admire the moon and the stars, often stopping to pray. They liked to pluck Kathleen from her bed and carry her with them.

Oswald's family may have lived in Zeitoun, but he journeyed to other camps and venues to lecture. Shortly after Miss Ashe's arrival, he began teaching a Wednesday night Bible class at Ezbekieh Gardens in Cairo; in March and early April he ministered to Tommies in YMCA huts along the Suez Canal. Given his travel during these months, Zeitoun management fell to Biddy. She led a Wednesday night League of Prayer–style prayer meeting in the marquee tent while he taught at Ezbekieh Gardens. Women, of course, had led the League of Prayer since 1916, so no one blinked at Biddy stepping in, particularly since she had done so in London. Plus, the soldiers enjoyed seeing an English-speaking woman in any capacity.

One April morning they noticed a change in the weather. The sky turned the color of copper as blowing wind from the Sahara Desert, on the western side of the Nile River, picked up speed. A short time later a *Khamin* wind tore through the camp at 140 mph, and the temperature rose twenty degrees. The humidity fell to 5 percent and the rough, sandy air sucked moisture from their skin.

The cyclone-force gusts blew down the center poles of the marquee tent and it ripped from top to bottom, collapsing into a canvas heap. Anything not tied down flew away. Sand drifts covered everything. But the adobe bungalow withstood all. By nightfall, the silty air caused a vivid sunset of red, purple, and gold.

Before Oswald could make arrangements to rebuild, the ANZAC troops stationed at Zeitoun received orders to new locations, many along the Suez Canal. With the camp suddenly emptied of soldiers, William Jessop asked Oswald to follow them to the area near Ismailia. Biddy, Mary Riley, and Kathleen required a permit to join him in a military zone, so Oswald requested permission, packed up his kit, and caught the train east.

While awaiting orders, Biddy and Mary closed the bungalow and, at the invitation of the Swan family, moved into the real house next door. The two families enjoyed each other's company, and Kathleen spent most of her days playing with David Swan anyway. The toddlers gamboled like happy puppies and wallowed in tubs of water to escape the Egyptian heat as summer drew near.

As he scrubbed Kathleen's back one day, David told Biddy, "When we get grown up, you'll be able to say, 'we washed each other's back in the bath,' won't you?"

Biddy tried not to smile. "Yes, I expect so."

David addressed himself to Kathleen's visiting father another day, reporting, "Kathleen and I are going to get married. She's going to be a nurse and I'm going to be a doctor. And we're going to be called Dr. and Mrs. Jones."[17]

Oswald thought the idea hilarious. (David did grow up to become a doctor, but he never changed his name.)

Without household chores or soldiers requiring attention, Biddy caught up on her letter writing and Oswald's diary entries. She typed her husband's scrawled notes and mailed them each month to Gertrude, who circulated copies to their BTC "family" as well as to actual relatives. Biddy's many correspondents demanded attention, and she wrote at least six letters every day, some typed and others in a looping handwriting that required vigilance not to swirl into shorthand.

Among those avid correspondents were Eva, Gladys, and Kathleen Ballinger, who awaited permission to join the Chamberses' YMCA work in Egypt. Since Biddy's departure Eva had acquired a serious suitor who concerned Gladys. She wrote with relief when Eva ended the relationship and recommitted herself to coming to Egypt. (Eva's grandson later volunteered that, to Eva, "Oswald Chambers represented everything ideal about a godly man which is probably why she traveled to Egypt."[18])

Gladys, for her part, still lived with her aging mother at Wimbledon and spent time with the brother of several of her in-laws, Vyvyan Donnithorne.[19] A talented engineer and Chinese linguist out of Cambridge, Donnithorne had set aside missionary plans for China to serve in the British Army. Injured in battle and sent home to recuperate, Vyvyan enjoyed talking with the pretty Gladys, and they shared a common concern for lost souls.

In early summer Oswald received a letter from Mrs. Reader Harris concerning the future of #45 Clapham Common and the Bible Training College. The League of Prayer had decided not to renew the lease on the building and to officially close down the school. In writing to Oswald, Mrs. Harris thanked him for his service but wanted to make sure he understood the League of Prayer had no further obligations to him or Biddy.

Since neither he nor Biddy expected anything from the League, the letter didn't trouble him beyond regret that Mrs. Harris felt compelled to spell it out. Indeed, that letter released Oswald and Biddy to dream about their future. Oswald floated an idea to friends about starting his own unaffiliated Bible college after the war. Biddy, of course, would handle the business end of any endeavor and supported the idea.

They had successfully run a school in England and now were gaining practical experience on a mission field filled with hardened men in a foreign country. Oswald and Biddy now better appreciated how to prepare prospective missionaries for overseas work. They knew personal discomfort and dangerous situations as well as the challenge of giving their utmost to God's purposes.

The reward?

God met their needs at every turn. He satisfied their lives with changed men, joyous experiences, beautiful sunrises, and fruitful work. Biddy filled notebooks with wisdom based on Oswald's teaching. Their daughter provided entertaining joy to men missing normal life.

Who knew what excitement the next six months of ministry would bring?

# 9

## The Destitution of Service

### *1916*

The real test of the saint is not preaching the gospel, but
washing disciples' feet.[1]

*L*etters flowed daily between the war zone and Zeitoun during May and June 1916, punctuated by the occasional need
for Oswald to visit YMCA headquarters in Cairo and thus stop
by to see his family.

Oswald knew his wife grew tired from the hard work of making a home in addition to her stenography and correspondence
duties. He welcomed this opportunity for Biddy to be "unbusy"
while staying with the Swans and advised her not to get flustered
by the long list of things she thought needed doing. Oswald told
Biddy and Miss Riley to rest, and Biddy took his words to heart.
Oswald soon saw the change, telling her, "I am profoundly grateful
that God tightened and bucked you up again."[2]

In addition to news, his letters spoke of his love and appreciation for Biddy. They show his ardor had not dimmed in the six years since their marriage in the Eltham garden. Their surroundings were vastly different but their love only burned deeper. As always, Oswald affirmed her value: "I have been refreshed deep down with . . . Macdonald's phrase, 'my wife's shielding heart.' A wife is not a chum or a comrade, anybody can be that, but a helpmeet—for she lives in God."[3]

It's not clear why the military took so long to authorize their passes, but Oswald believed God controlled even the decision-making powers of the ANZAC armies: "In God's good time we will be together again and I do not want it before His good time and neither do you."[4]

Assigned to a small New Zealand camp near Ismailia rather than the sprawling Australian Moascar camp, Oswald set to work building a YMCA hut of native mats. There, the men could write letters, participate in prayer meetings, and listen to his evening talks on the Sermon on the Mount. Temperatures inside the soldiers' canvas tents often rose to 130 degrees during the day, making the airy YMCA huts a comparative respite from the debilitating heat.

A colonial city located at the midpoint of the forty-five-year-old Suez Canal, Ismailia marked where the train tracks turned north. The Suez Canal Authority headquartered there in an arched and domed building along the waterfront. Designed in French Colonial style, the European section featured graceful tree-lined boulevards and public gardens, an oasis from the rough desert spreading along the canal to Port Said.

ANZAC troops around Ismailia guarded the Suez Canal as well as trained for planned battles across the Sinai. The intrepid Miss Ashe described the situation for the soldiers as "one of utter strain and deprivation. . . . Ineptitude bore heavily upon them; the pitiless heat, the fierce relentless sun, the scorching sand, the insects—the flies and swarming insatiable mosquitoes—bore hard upon their courage and endurance."[5]

Jessop sent YMCA secretaries to meet both spiritual and physical refreshment needs—lime juice kept cool in ice chests was very popular in the desert. Both Jimmy Hanson and Philip Hancock served with mobile units along the canal that summer. The YMCA's Lord Radstock described camp secretaries like Chambers, Hanson, and Hancock as "often single-handed, overworked, not too well-nourished, [enduring] very long hours, intense heat, sand, dirt and flies."[6]

While Biddy, Miss Riley, and Kathleen stayed in Zeitoun, Oswald roomed with Ashley King's family of the Ismailia branch of the EGM. The EGM sponsored a school for girls in the town and, like the Swans, the Kings lived in a roomy two-story house. They had prayed Jessop would send the Chambers family to Ismailia and welcomed Oswald. In fact, they invited the whole family to stay with them.

On Saturday, July 1, Oswald got the message from YMCA headquarters he had been waiting for: "Cheers, meet the 9:20 train."[7]

Delighted to be reunited with his family again, Oswald had a surprise announcement for his wife and Miss Riley at the train station: he had decided to close the small YMCA refreshment canteen on the morrow (where they charged Tommies a pittance for refreshments) and instead serve a free tea from two to five o'clock in the afternoon.

Welcome to Ismailia, ladies!

Both Biddy and Oswald disapproved of using a "bait and switch" method to lure people into a church service. They preferred to practice hospitality by providing a free tea and allowing the Holy Spirit to inspire a thirst for truth.

Fortunately, the granddaughter of two master bakers did not have to bake her first weekend in Ismailia. An English friend had sent £5 to sponsor the refreshments (US $450, 2014),[8] so Oswald purchased the needed baked goods from the YMCA-operated bakery in Port Said.

From the Kings' Ismailia home, they drove to camp along an avenue of orange-blossomed acacia trees, past the blue water of the wide canal and into the scorching sweep of tawny sand northwest of town. The camp spread before them: white tents, rugged wagons, metal artillery, and tail-flicking horses. The brand-new YMCA mat hut stood on the edge of the camp, its distinctive red triangle sign marking the spot.

The two women made the hut as inviting as possible on such short notice. Biddy spread a red baize cloth over a table and set out literature: copies of the League of Prayer's *Tongues of Fire* magazine, pamphlets of Oswald's talks, a few books, and a pile of khaki-colored pocket New Testaments provided by the YMCA.

Miss Riley sorted the food with the help of several soldier volunteers. They covered everything because of the flies. The lime drinks remained in the coolers until required, but fired-up urns soon steeped tea.

The afternoon sun scorched in the still air. At two o'clock men streamed from the camp to the hut. Some gaped in surprise at the British women in wide-brimmed hats serving tea, but even more grinned, teeth white against tanned faces, to see a beautifully dressed three-year-old with a large bow in her hair helping her father direct traffic.

"Where do we pay?" asked a soldier.

"Have you got cigarettes or tinned fruit?" called another.

"All we have today are tea and cakes," Oswald said. "Nothing is for sale, but you may have all the cookies and tea you like."

Far from home and rarely granted time away from camp, to the soldiers the prospect of being able to sit at rest in an airy hut seemed a dream. The flies remained ever constant, and whisks never lagged, but for a short time war worries receded and they could be men without fear, a cup of tea and a plateful of cookies at their side. The Tommies loved it.

They served four hundred soldiers that day.

The troops returned to camp by five o'clock, though several remained behind to help with cleanup, which involved packing the cups and plates for washing at the Kings' home.

Exhausted though she may have been, Biddy had much to ponder as she completed her tasks. The soldiers had been full of training stories and concerns about the battlefield. Some grieved the death of friends, others griped about the conditions and hard work. But most men were grateful for the YMCA's refreshments, Biddy and Miss Riley's service, and sweet Kathleen's chatter. Many stopped to tell her specifically of their thankfulness for Oswald: "God's man in God's place."[9]

The following week, however, YMCA officials grumbled about the precedent Oswald had set by giving away food. An official group journeyed to Ismailia to discuss the issue.

After meeting with Oswald and hearing the soldiers' gratitude, officials permitted Oswald to continue providing free Sunday teas as long as he received £20 in donations to cover expenses. (Oswald estimated they could serve tea to two thousand men for each £5.) Two members of the YMCA staff attending the meeting donated £5 each, and the rest of the funds arrived immediately in the mail. Oswald agreed to put out a box for donations to cover costs, just as he did with pamphlets in the Zeitoun hut, and no one objected to free teas again.

Out in the desert every Sunday afternoon, Biddy and Miss Riley toiled to make the men feel comfortable. They served traditional refreshments, even creating fruit trifle. (Disappointment occurred one morning, however, when ants penetrated the chest for their own sampling of the English treat.)

Miss Riley took Kathleen with her to shop for supplies early in the morning. The English woman relished bargaining with native sellers and Kathleen enjoyed the market chaos. Biddy stayed home to catch up on secretarial tasks.

Evenings found Biddy in the Ismailia hut, taking down Oswald's words verbatim into her latest notebook. In addition to the Sermon on the Mount, he also lectured from the biblical ethics curriculum he had developed for the correspondence course. Once she closed her notebook and set aside her pencil, she watched earnest soldiers besiege him with questions—both friendly and hostile. Oswald liked to end the evenings by telling the men, "Whether you agree with what I've said is a matter of moonshine as long as you begin to think."[10] He enjoyed the give-and-take with men who disagreed with him.

In his element, Oswald radiated enthusiasm, joy, and interest in each soldier. He had one aim: to get men in touch with Jesus Christ. His Sermon on the Mount talks emphasized the pertinence of Jesus's words to twentieth-century life, even within the army. One soldier told him, "It has been worthwhile enlisting to come to these classes."[11]

Oswald's practical examples never downplayed the importance of the gospel, and he took time to make sure the men understood. It was the power of the gospel, after all, that enabled him to teach with such assurance, never losing sight of his absolute trust in his Lord and what he could do.

Biddy shared his confidence. Stripped of all luxuries and battling mosquitoes in the savage heat, she could have grumbled often and no one would have been surprised. But Biddy chose to look at events from God's point of view in every situation of her life. God had set her, Oswald, Miss Riley, and Kathleen in this time and place. His grace would be sufficient to meet their needs.

All the same, Oswald recognized the strain placed on a woman used to city life. As he wrote Biddy in a note of encouragement, "I am unfathomably thankful to you and to God again with the leisure that I may be broken bread and poured out wine for the multitude. This means sacrifice for you, not in glorious ways but . . . the hardest ways."[12]

As summer drew to a close, Oswald and Biddy started to look for a place to stay long-term in Ismailia, since so many troops were stationed along the canal. But in early September Jessop wrote to announce ANZAC forces were opening a School of Instruction at Zeitoun and he would need them back in October.

The bungalow still stood, but Jessop decided to replace the marquee hut. In keeping with other YMCA centers in Egypt, he arranged to build a canteen hut as well, thus increasing the ministry opportunities within the EGM compound. He suggested the Chambers family take a holiday at the end of September while the new huts were being constructed.

The day before departing Ismailia, Oswald and Jimmy Hanson met the SS *Medina* at Port Said. The long-awaited trio of Eva, Gladys, and Kathleen Ballinger had finally arrived to work in Egypt. They escorted the beaming young women to Ismailia for a reunion at the EGM house.

Little Kathleen, Miss Riley, and Biddy were thrilled to see rosy and laughing Eva, Kathleen Ballinger with calm, shining eyes, and Gladys sporting a new ring. They spent the joyful reunion praising God and telling of their adventures. Biddy apprised them of female life in Egypt and everyone recounted tales of working with the soldiers. The BTC Expeditionary Force lacked only Philip Hancock and Miss Ashe that night.

The three women planned to work with Miss Ashe at the Alexandria Soldier's Home not far from the sea. Since the Chambers family planned a ten-day holiday nearby, Biddy and Kathleen traveled with them the next morning to Alexandria. Oswald and Miss Riley would catch up a few days later after checking on Zeitoun's construction projects.

Once on their way, the women turned their attention to personal matters. After nine months spent with soldiers, Biddy wanted to hear the real concerns in the young women's hearts.

While everyone had watched Kathleen Ballinger with deliberately innocent faces the night before, Biddy laughed when the young woman casually asked on the train, "Any real news of Phil?" Biddy assured her of Secretary Hancock's excitement over her arrival in Egypt. When he left for Egypt, Philip had released his hopes of a future with Kathleen to God—and now God was reuniting them.

Biddy pointed to the Donnithorne family crest engraved on Gladys's new ring and asked for the full story. The blushing woman had become engaged before leaving England and Vyvyan Donnithorne, worried a jeweled ring might tempt theft, gave Gladys a simple gold ring to wear. Since she had promised to join the BTC crew in Egypt before she fell in love, Gladys saw no reason to change her mind despite having a beau at home.

As for Eva, the merry twenty-three-year-old merely looked out the window and asked, "Met any promising soldiers?"

The laughter in the midst of a hot summer day during a war on a foreign continent cheered Biddy's hardworking soul. The presence of these women she loved and trusted was a blessing she had only hoped for.

The balmy air off the Mediterranean Sea refreshed them after the hot blasts of interior Egypt. While they visited at the Soldier's Home and attended Oswald's evening services there, Biddy and Miss Riley spent most days relaxing. They picnicked by the ocean, wearing sun-shielding floppy hats, and little Kathleen wore a knee-length jumpsuit with short sleeves when she waded in the water. A photo caught both Biddy and Oswald sitting on seaside rocks with books in hand.

The family returned to a changed Zeitoun compound in October 1916. Workmen had erected a freestanding wooden roof over the bungalow and extended it almost double the length to shelter an outdoor cooking area. They also added a deep veranda to the front of the bungalow to provide a shaded and more defined area for tables and chairs. In addition, workers had constructed a refreshment canteen, a mud-brick kitchen, storehouses, and a study hut with room for fifty people.

A standard YMCA hut now stood on the site of the marquee tent. Built of native matting nailed to a wooden frame, the hut stretched seventy feet long by forty feet wide, and was thirty-five feet tall with matted window openings high up for ventilation. Inside, an organ and a podium shared a wooden platform. Bare electric lightbulbs hung from the ceiling the length of the hut, and sand made up the floor. Four hundred wooden folding chairs lined up facing the stage or surrounded trestle tables, with enough open space for an additional hundred to stand.

Oswald posted a large wooden sign near the YMCA compound entrance advertising the study hut (also called the devotional hut), open 9:00 a.m. to 9:00 p.m., designed for reading, writing, and study. The hut also featured a blackboard lecture at 7:30 in the evening. The subject one night? "Religious Problems Raised by the War."

Biddy surveyed the changes and wrote to *Tongues of Fire* magazine, "It has been very wonderful to watch it develop bit by bit until now it is quite a YM settlement and the men are keenly appreciative of it all."[13]

The new School of Instruction ran eight-week classes to train officers in specialized skills necessary for war. Hundreds of soldiers now rotated through the camp, providing even more men for Oswald to mentor. The camp hummed with activity.

Oswald focused his evening talks on subjects the soldiers feared as the war dragged on. Up to fifty men—and the note-taking Biddy—crowded into the study hut five nights a week while he discussed issues such as the problem of suffering. William Jessop, who stopped in now and then, noted the subjects were "treated from a Biblical standpoint and . . . so handled that each lecture is complete in itself. He packs into each lesson what most people would spread over two or three."[14]

Oswald wrote out an alliterative outline on the blackboard prior to each lecture. Before class, men gathered to discuss the Scripture references and debate the meaning of the headings and subheadings. Oswald frequently underscored a right relationship to Jesus Christ as being the only ground for their spiritual confidence.

On the sixth night of the week, Oswald reviewed the previous five lessons and took questions. Sundays were reserved for the general service in the large hut, which included singing hymns and standing-room-only crowds.

They used the YMCA hymnbook and, accompanied by the pump organ, regularly sang such favorites as "For All the Saints from Whom Their Labors Rest," "The Hope and Coming of the Lord," "O Love That Will Not Let Me Go," and "Ten Thousand Times Ten Thousand." Everyone soon learned the verbal shorthand for Biddy's favorite hymn to close the evenings, "SYL 494," ("See you later, page number 494"), a reference to the song "God Be with You Till We Meet Again."

Most gratifying of all, soldiers formed small study groups within their units to discuss and study God's Word once they returned to the front lines.

Life had fallen into a routine when Gladys unexpectedly arrived from Alexandria, mourning the loss of her physician brother, Thomas, at the Somme. Biddy welcomed her with open arms to grieve. The first night, Oswald and Biddy took her out to the desert to admire the stars and full moon and held Gladys to their hearts.

While they sat to listen and weep with Gladys, the family also took her on local outings. They traveled into Cairo and sampled ice cream at Groppi's. They rode camelback to the pyramids. They even visited the narrow granite obelisk known as Cleopatra's Needle, along with the Virgin's Well near Heliopolis—allegedly the spot where Mary, Joseph, and Jesus rested on their flight to Egypt.

When Gladys returned to Alexandria, Eva moved to Zeitoun. Australian nurses were taking over their work at the Alexandria hospital and Biddy could use Eva's assistance at the YMCA camp. They built Eva a small mat hut near the bungalow and she stepped into service.

The canteen addition provided more opportunities to serve the soldiers. YMCA canteens at the time sold items at reasonable prices: a cup of tea, coffee, or cocoa cost half a *piastre* (the lowest Egyptian coin); a plate of stewed fruit cost one *piastre*; three fried eggs and potato chips cost two and a half *piastres*. The tiny profits funded games, writing paper, lime juice, and similar items for men on the front lines. Being close to Cairo, Zeitoun's canteen also could supply ice cream, which the soldiers ate by the gallons in the brutal heat.[15]

The success of Ismailia's free teas convinced Oswald and Biddy they should provide the same on Sundays at Zeitoun. Monetary gifts arrived from England and, with the convenience of YMCA stores readily available in Cairo, Biddy and Miss Riley made arrangements.

Biddy focused on hospitality and how to make the huts feel more home-like. She spread white tablecloths on the square tables and placed a vase with a flower in the middle of each. With the new kitchen, Biddy and Miss Riley expanded the menu to include sandwiches, fried eggs, fruit salad, trifle, ice cream, cake, and drinks—and five to seven hundred soldiers stopped by for tea on Sundays.

Jessop spoke highly of Biddy and Miss Riley's efforts, particularly in their effect on the men. "Their 'bit' has been equal to that of the Secretaries and the dainty touches given by them have meant more to the soldiers than we realize."[16]

Oswald, meanwhile, spent Sundays preaching. He began at the Zeitoun hut early in the morning, walked a mile across the desert to the Aotea Convalescent Home for a service, returned to Zeitoun for a communion service at noon, and spent the evenings at Ezbekieh Gardens for one more talk.

An evening meal followed his return, and those visitors remaining sang hymns and prayed together. Oswald liked to remind them God kept open house for the universe, and he—and the Chambers family—welcomed everyone. Conversation around the table included current events, books (Oswald liked Rider Haggard's novels), and the latest news from home.

The year 1916 ended with a satisfying ministry, dear friends, and the privilege of seeing God's hand at work in the lives of men facing the possibility of death. The war ground on across France, and military action ramped up in the Sinai. Many BTC friends wore uniforms, and so many families struggled to make sense of casualties. Surely, the war could not last much longer—could it?

Oswald wrote a simple message of encouragement on the blackboard for the midnight watch service on December 31: "Finish, 1916." When the clock struck midnight, he turned over the blackboard to read: "1917, A great New Year to you all. 'And God shall wipe away all tears.' Revelation 21:4."[17]

They looked forward to seeing how God would bring his Word to pass.

# 10

## The Teaching of Adversity

### *1917*

God . . . gives strength . . . only for the strain of the minute.[1]

O swald liked to post provocative statements on the small blackboard outside the study hut. One day he wrote, "Beware! There is a religious talk here each evening!" When a January monsoon flooded the camp, he scribbled: "Closed during submarine maneuvers."[2] Without soldiers tromping through the wet sand and wild rain over the next several days, Oswald enjoyed a needed rest. With his long hours and persistent call to minister, he spent a lot of time away from his wife and daughter.

Biddy focused on camp-related tasks: the canteen, taking dictation, writing letters, supervising Kathleen, mentoring the BTC women, and typing up Oswald's notes. Their day together still began in the early dawn hours with the *Daily Light* reading, prayer, and a cup of tea followed by Oswald's studies while Biddy attended to Kathleen. Other people filled their days, but they remained mindful of each other.

Oswald took meticulous care of his uniform and shined his shoes—he believed dressing well showed professionalism and respect to others. He also didn't want Biddy to look merely neat and tidy; he wanted her to look well-dressed. Whenever he found extra money in his pocket, he took Biddy into Cairo for personal shopping—often a new hat.

During the fourth year of a war, while living in a camp, Biddy daily wore a light shirtwaist, dark skirt, and laced boots. She brushed her wavy hair into a knot at the base of her neck, though after a long hot day curly tendrils always escaped.

Other than during her trips to the seashore, photos of Kathleen always show her in a neatly pressed dress. Whenever Biddy glimpsed her daughter's clothing in disarray, she stopped to straighten her skirt. Oswald relished taking his daughter to Cairo's posh Shepheard's Hotel beauty salon to have her hair done with a big white bow.

A special outing for the camp's Englishwomen meant catching the tram into Cairo's center. They'd stop at Groppi's, poke around in the Muski—the big market—and bring home treats to share with their visitors. They also enjoyed the Giza Zoo, not far from the ancient Sphinx. More than once Biddy and Oswald visited the pyramids after dark on a camel tour made even more romantic by a golden moon and countless stars.

Biddy soon developed a friendship with Amy Zwemer, the wife of Samuel Zwemer, a longtime American missionary expert on Islam. Twenty years older than Biddy and with teenaged daughters, Amy had lived an adventurous life following her brilliant husband on missionary forays around the world. As the family lived in an upstairs apartment not far from Groppi's and welcomed callers, the Chambers family often stopped by.

Despite her busy parents, Kathleen's life overflowed with loving and attentive adults. The little girl reigned as a princess in the soldiers' hearts. They bestowed affection, playtime, and gifts on the precocious child.

Among Kathleen's favorites was Australian Peter Kay. A hard-drinking, hard-living man with plenty of women on the side, Peter came to know God one day at the devotional hut. As he explained, "When I realized what Almighty God had done for me, I realized I would be a cad if I didn't own Him as my Lord and Master."[3] He doted on Kathleen. She, in turn, thought him the "cat's whiskers" when he spent all his free time and leave at Zeitoun.

The Chambers family lost track of Peter when his unit left for the front lines. Several mutual friends later visited Zeitoun on leave and approached Oswald with their concerns: "You think Peter Kay's a Christian, don't you? He may know God, but he's doing the same things he did before."

Oswald heard them out before replying, "The Holy Spirit will teach him and by degrees, those things will drop off like dead leaves, and he won't do them anymore."[4]

The men shook their heads, but when Kay realized the error of his ways, he did indeed stop. On their next visit, the soldiers admitted Oswald's wisdom.

A wild-looking man who preferred to wear an Outback slouch hat on his head and a scarf around his neck, Peter Kay brought Kathleen a donkey in January 1917. Over the next few days he and his mates supervised the three-and-a-half-year-old kicking the donkey's sides as she rode around the compound. Biddy and Oswald watched the riding lessons and ordered another animal pen to be built. They posted a sign: *"Eshat el Homar"* (Hut of the Donkey).

That spring Kathleen played with four kittens in addition to chasing after John Silence—a large panther-like cat who presided over the compound like a phantom. Various dogs came and went, along with tortoises, lizards, doves, and pigeons—which were housed in a dovecote high on a pole. Also, Reverend Douglas Downes often left his friendly brown-and-white collie, Patsy, for a visit.

Kathleen attended her father's Sunday services and sang with gusto. Most evenings Biddy tucked the little girl into bed before picking up her pencil to take down Oswald's lecture. Tommies often asked to observe the sleeping child. They gently touched Kathleen's hair and whispered a prayer. Men missing their own children would smile as she prattled about childish affairs. For a few moments they could close their eyes and imagine domestic life back home.

Biddy created a homey oasis within the Zeitoun camp where visitors could come and go, feeling welcomed and apart from the war. Perhaps she remembered Emily Hobbs filling the Woolwich and Eltham houses with visitors for tea, stories, and comfort. With her husband's encouragement and participation, Biddy did the same in the desert.

Even soldiers who didn't subscribe to Oswald's teaching felt welcome. Private Stephen Pulford's story is a classic example.

Not wanting anything to do with religious people, Pulford visited Zeitoun only to buy refreshments and write letters. After a few visits, he voiced his surprise that no one was forcing their religious beliefs upon him. A fellow Tommie suggested he attend one of Oswald's lectures, assuring Pulford no one would quiz him on the state of his soul.

He found the talks interesting but wasn't converted. Pulford continued to stop by the YMCA camp when he felt like it but carefully avoided close contact with Oswald, Biddy, or the BTC women.

After a while, however, "the openhearted welcome I received overcame my reserve and their bungalow became a home away from home. Any soldier will tell of the relief to escape a barrack room atmosphere into civilian surrounds," Pulford recounted. When he returned on leave for a visit, he became as "one of the family, during which time I was, no doubt, subconsciously absorbing a way of life which was new to me. Not once, however, was I approached on spiritual matters; if I had been, it might have put me off forever."[5]

With the increased activity at the camp, William Jessop reassigned Jimmy Hanson to Zeitoun as well. A friendly secretary with a hearty laugh, Jimmy filled in and ensured the ministry continued without problems whenever Oswald lectured elsewhere. Gladys joined them to work at the canteen full time, while Miss Ashe and Kathleen Ballinger left Alexandria to run a small YMCA hut beside the tracks at the Benha train station. There, the two British women provided hot tea, sandwiches, stewed fruit, and eggs to the soldiers changing trains an hour north of Cairo. They also held Thursday night and Sunday morning services for men stationed at the nearby Benha garrison.

Philip Hancock traveled to Zeitoun whenever the opportunity arose, particularly if he could rendezvous with Kathleen Ballinger. The YMCA stationed the short secretary in a forward YMCA hut from which he ministered to troops training for the Sinai assault.

Oswald taught on the book of Job that spring, believing it significant to the men attending his classes. They daily worked with weapons, witnessed their friends' deaths, and knew the carnage awaiting them. The men longed for encouragement and consolation in the face of a never-ending, grinding, grim war.

Oswald described Job's life as a "heartbreaking devotion to God in the midst of inexplicable complexity of sorrow." He saw the book as a consolation because of Job's understanding of human suffering. "No attempt is made to explain the why of suffering, but rather an expression is given to suffering which leaves one with the inspiration of an explanation in the final issue."[6]

Owing to troop movements and the short class schedules at the School of Instruction, soldiers often couldn't attend an entire lecture series. That, coupled with strong interest, spurred Biddy to turn her Job notes into a manuscript suitable for publication.

Biddy transcribed her swirls, dots, curves, and lines into typed words. She edited the typewritten pages, correcting grammar and smoothing out Oswald's sentences to make them clearer. Biddy retyped the pages until they were perfect.

The responsibility for the manuscript fell completely to her. In a letter to friends in England, Oswald wrote, "[I] hope to send you a book on Job soon (at least Biddy does, I take no more responsibility after having spoken my mind)."[7]

Biddy took the pages to the Nile Mission Press in Cairo and they returned the proofs in August. Biddy and Oswald examined the sheets together, looking for misprints and adjusting awkward sentences before sending them back for publication.

The title, *Baffled to Fight Better*, came from the poem "Asolando" by Robert Browning, Oswald's favorite poet. The poem quoted in the epilogue suggests how Oswald admired the soldiers under his spiritual care:

> One who never turned his back but marched
> >    breast forward
> Never doubted clouds would break
> Never dreamed, though right were worsted,
> >    wrong would triumph
> Held we fall to rise
> are baffled to fight better
> Sleep to wake.[8]

Meanwhile, when Oswald agreed to travel to Alexandria once a week to teach (a three-hour train ride each way), Biddy took over his Thursday night class. With her years of experience taking down the messages, coupled with his detailed outlines, she stepped into the role with aplomb.

The scope of Biddy's responsibilities widened even as they became more complicated by having pretty British girls to mentor in an army camp. Her general letters were sent to anyone interested on the front lines; in camps, hospitals, and convalescent homes throughout the war theater; home to England; and even Australia. Miss Ashe noted, "The amount of actual work they represent and the miracle of the time found to do them—and the joy with which they were done is fine to recall."[9]

Biddy could not have accomplished the task without the young BTC women. The capable Gladys took responsibility for the canteen's cash box and oversaw the orderlies and native helpers. She helped prepare food, and a photo exists of Gladys demonstrating the bread slicer to Oswald. Her smiling face drew the men to Zeitoun's canteen, and they later returned to hear her sing in the evening services.

Eva spent most of her time working in the bungalow and helping with Kathleen's care. A sensitive young woman, she kept a prayer journal during her time in Egypt. In September 1917, she wrote, "O, Lord, Thou knowest what a chaos it all seems sometimes," before acknowledging nothing mattered as long as it was in his will.[10] Soldiers gathered about to hear her merry laugh, and she attracted the particular attention of "Tim," a nickname for Stephen Pulford.

Kathleen Ballinger and Miss Ashe often escaped the frazzling Benha workload by weekend visits to Zeitoun. When Kathleen fell seriously ill in the summer of 1917 and nearly died, she recuperated at the bungalow for several weeks. Philip got leave to visit, wrote her father for permission, and asked her to marry him. Once she was healthy again, Kathleen and Philip returned to their respective duty stations—engaged.

Jimmy Hanson received permission to return to England in August to marry another former BTC student, Florence Gudgin. The two hoped to return together, but with the escalating war tempo, they were unsure "Gudgie" could travel back with her new husband. Jimmy would return in December, with or without her.

The women's cheery efficiency in the canteen prompted a request from the instructors assigned to the School of Instruction next door. These officers asked if they could pay Biddy and her crew to provide an officer's "mess" (a dining room and meals) for twenty-five officers at noon and in the evening.

With Eva and Gladys available to help, Biddy and Miss Riley agreed "with their usual spirit of helpfulness," according to William

Jessop, who authorized such use of the YMCA's facility. The women did the cooking themselves, to great applause from the men. Jessop received thanks and compliments, and laughed when one officer said he would "forgo the comfort of a chair and sit on the sand to get such a meal."[11]

Though often traveling between stations to teach, Oswald was kept apprised of the women's toil under arduous conditions. "It takes some vitality, morally, physically and spiritually to be cheerful in weather like today [following a sandstorm that covered the compound in deep sand]."[12]

The soldiers saw the sacrifices the women made to serve them and provide pleasant surroundings. Dozens volunteered in the canteen or other huts to keep things in order. They joined the family after supper for hymns and prayers shared under the star-filled sky. "Zeitoun is the hub of the universe to us," one explained.[13] The Chambers family felt the same. As Biddy wrote to the League of Prayer members: "We always retire with the sense that it has been another day full of the presence and blessing of God."[14]

And so the year went by, punctuated by a five-day trip to the seashore at Damietta—the only holiday the family took in 1917.

For a respite from the broiling Egyptian sun, Oswald arranged for the construction of a dugout at Zeitoun that summer. Buried half in the ground with the top half constructed of thick adobe bricks, it squatted near the bungalow and provided a quiet, relatively cooler place to study and prepare his lectures. From there he wrote letters, including this one to Emily Hobbs:

> As for Biddy I love her and I am her husband but I do not believe it is possible to exaggerate what she has been in the way of a Sacrament out here—God conveying His presence through the common elements of an ordinary life. The letters she has received from mothers and wives and sisters and fathers and brothers are in themselves a deep testimony to a most unconscious ministry of wife and mother and woman.

Of the other women, what can I say? Never, I think, did any man have such a unique privilege as I have had in being associated with such women.[15]

A new avenue for ministry opened that summer at the Aotea Convalescent Home, and Oswald taught out of Jeremiah, including a talk on "A Poetical View of Appendicitis." At first skeptical when Oswald began his afternoon treks across the sand, the hospital matron soon recognized the positive results of his visits on her patients. She undoubtedly noticed, however, the climate's physical effect on the YMCA secretary.

Oswald's already thin frame now required several new notches in his belt. His uniform hung on his shoulders and his eyes appeared sunken in a lined, mahogany face. With so much to do for the soldiers—changes were afoot as the soldiers trained for General Allenby's final push to Jerusalem—he didn't seem to notice the toll on his own body. While William Jessop advised his secretaries to rest in the afternoons, Oswald continued to visit hospitals.

Jessop soon brought Dr. Gilbert Deaver, an American physician now assigned to the YMCA, out to Zeitoun to meet Oswald and Biddy. The ANZAC high command wanted at least one YMCA secretary at each casualty clearing station once the fighting began. Jessop thought to pair Oswald with Deaver. Once the winter rains started, fighting would begin. Biddy wrote the news in a letter to her mother and Dais:

> So when you read of the "taking" of Gaza in the papers you'll know that he'll be up amongst the wounded men and mighty glad he'll be to be there. . . . We shall carry on here as well as may be, rather like walking about with your head cut off![16]

Eager to join the men he taught as they faced battle, Oswald arranged for his desert kit. Biddy taught more classes, a new chaplain named Mr. Watson arrived to help, and Oswald made arrangements for others to come as necessary. George Swan could take a class, for example, or Samuel Zwemer. Oswald left everything in place for the work to carry on without him. Once the orders came, he could go without concern.

However, Oswald returned one Wednesday night from Ezbekieh Gardens not feeling well. Intestinal and stomach ailments were frequent in Egypt, particularly with the ever-present insects. He couldn't sleep and had no appetite. A fierce pain stabbed his side. Exhausted, Oswald rested and read. When Biddy and others urged him to visit the Red Cross hospital at Giza, he demurred.

They all knew General Allenby had finally sent his soldiers to battle in Gaza and southern Palestine. The army expected severe casualties—and Oswald refused to go to the doctor lest he require a hospital bed an injured soldier might need. His concerned wife and colleagues disagreed, but he remained stubborn.

On Monday, October 29, twelve days after his illness began, the pain became unbearable and Oswald finally agreed to see a doctor. A car took Biddy and a moaning Oswald to the hospital. An army surgeon examined him and immediately ordered Oswald into emergency surgery for a ruptured appendix. Biddy waited in a chair supplied by a sympathetic matron and held her Bible close. She prayed.

"A success," the doctor announced when he found her. But in an age before antibiotics, the biggest concern was infection and frail Oswald's ability to fight off sepsis. They must wait and pray.

Biddy arranged to stay with Oswald and sent a message to Zeitoun in time for the evening class. Soldiers knelt on the hut's sandy floor to pray for Oswald's recovery.

She never left his bedside. The exhausted forty-three-year-old Oswald dozed and appeared to be gaining strength and recovering. But on November 4, a blood clot developed in his lung. Doctors found another the following day. Oswald fell unconscious. Prayers continued.

Biddy searched her Bible and prayed, focusing on and repeating the verse God impressed upon her mind: "This sickness is not unto death." The words belonged to Jesus in John 11:4, referring to Lazarus's death at Bethany. Given the importance and magnitude of Oswald's work at Zeitoun, God surely could not call him home?

"I'm so sorry, Mrs. Chambers," a nurse said, "but he cannot recover from this."

Biddy shook her head, remembering that word.

YMCA officials and friends stopped by. Oswald regained consciousness and seemed better. Biddy sent word for Kathleen to visit.

When the four-and-a-half-year-old strode into the room, Oswald brightened but lacked energy. He whispered, "Hello, Scallywag," before falling against his pillow.

The plucky Kathleen described the latest events at Zeitoun with her animals and kissed him. A nurse then declared the visit over.

Wasted from illness, Oswald nevertheless kept Biddy's hopes alive by rallying and regaining strength.

A week after Kathleen's visit, however, his lungs hemorrhaged.

On November 15, 1917, at seven o'clock in the morning, Oswald Chambers died.

# 11

## What Is That to Thee?

### *November 1917*

Realize the danger of being an amateur providence.[1]

From the Red Cross hospital, Biddy traveled to Amy Zwemer's downtown Cairo home. Amy hugged Biddy, listened, and wept with her. When her husband, Samuel, came in, the three prayed together. Psalm 142:7 came to Biddy's mind and comforted her: "Bring my soul out of prison, that I may praise thy name: the righteous shall compass me about; for thou shalt deal bountifully with me."

It was still early in the day.

At Biddy's request, a sorrowing William Jessop sent cables to Biddy's family, as well as Oswald's parents, his brother, and Mrs. Reader Harris. The simple message: "Oswald in His Presence."

The hardest task that morning lay ahead, once Biddy had calmed herself; she had to break the news to her little girl at Zeitoun.

"My mother came back to the bungalow and she picked me up," Kathleen remembered years later. "She said, 'Your daddy's gone to be with Jesus.'"

"Well, that's wonderful, isn't it?" the child Kathleen said. "What are you crying for?"

It was the only time Kathleen ever saw her mother cry. "She never did. She was always so determined that God never made a mistake."[2]

Perhaps Biddy lay down to take a nap in her own bed for the first time in weeks. Perhaps she answered a million questions, or none at all. Certainly Eva and Gladys hugged her, undoubtedly crying. Tears would flavor Mary Riley's soup that night and likely for days to come.

Soon a message came from Samuel Zwemer. Dr. and Mrs. Phillips of the American Mission had room on their ship, the *Ibis*, currently moored in Luxor. Kathleen and Biddy were welcome, along with a friend, to spend a week on board to grieve.

William Jessop also came to Zeitoun with an immediate question for Biddy. The ANZAC command requested Oswald have a full military funeral the next day. They asked to bury him at the Old Cairo cemetery with the soldiers he loved.

Burials usually took place the day of death in Egypt, and that's probably what Biddy expected. But Oswald felt such a kinship with the soldiers he would have appreciated this sign of their affection for him. She needed to weigh how God could best be glorified in this stunning moment.

Throughout their time together, Biddy never had Oswald only to herself. In his life as well as his death, she shared him with many others. She knew those who loved and respected Oswald felt abandoned and possibly distraught that God let him die.

She agreed to the unusual honor.

What next?

Oswald's teaching was plain: when you were not sure what God wanted, examine the situation and your options and then do the next logical thing. Biddy thanked Mr. Zwemer for contacting Dr. and Mrs. Phillips, then asked Eva to accompany her and Kathleen to Luxor.

She knew their Zeitoun friends needed to mourn together, even as she craved privacy. But the camp must function, so Biddy made decisions and wrote directions. She packed her suitcase and, after prayers that night, walked into the desert to gaze at the stars once more, remembering.

The next morning a car called for Biddy, Kathleen, Eva, and their luggage. They traveled to the Red Cross hospital to join the military funeral procession. Oswald's flag-draped coffin lay on a caisson drawn by six black horses. Three officers rode and six officers marched alongside. Biddy and the others traveled immediately behind in a closed black car.

An open car followed with senior officers. Behind them one hundred more officers trekked, their rifles slung backward over their shoulders as befitted a military burial. The line of men stretched as far as Biddy could see.

The procession started from the hospital, marched across the Nile River bridges, and continued a mile through the twisting streets of Old Cairo to the cemetery. They skirted a high stone wall to the cemetery entrance. There, the six officers escorting the caisson muscled the wooden casket onto their broad shoulders and shuffled through the gate.

Biddy nodded to the people gathered outside the walls: men and women, civilians and military members, the elevator man from the YMCA building, and even their native foreman. She followed the casket into the cemetery past rows of rough wooden crosses marking soldiers' graves. Oswald's pallbearers maneuvered the casket into place beside a mound of dirt while several rows of mourning men and women gathered around the open grave. All the Cairo YMCA personnel attended.

Kathleen clutched Biddy's hand and stared at the crying people, the open grave, the many uniformed men, and faces she knew well.

Samuel Zwemer read the burial service. A bugler played "The Last Post." The rifles fired.

Soldiers removed the flag and lowered the casket into the ground. The service ended.

Mary Riley thought the impressive military service one of joyous victory, manifesting the "wonderful undertaking of God."[3]

Before Biddy left, William Jessop stopped her. "Will you stay to carry on at Zeitoun until the end of the war? Think and pray about it while you are gone. I would like you to stay."

She considered him a long moment, then scanned the faces of the other mourners. Yes, she would pray and think about it. Biddy joined Kathleen and Eva in the car. At the station they departed for the fourteen-hour, 450-mile trip to Luxor on the overnight train.

Like all Europeans, they traveled first class in a sleeping car. Once the train's novelty wore off, Kathleen fell asleep, leaving Biddy and Eva to grieve together.

Eva was the obvious choice to accompany Biddy, as Kathleen Ballinger and Miss Ashe were busy at Benha, Gladys ran the canteen, and Miss Riley oversaw the cooking. As the most sensitive and emotional, Eva perhaps craved Biddy's presence as much as the new widow needed her sympathetic ear. The two could cry together.

In the morning, Dr. H. E. Phillips and his wife met them at the Luxor train station and escorted them to the *Ibis*, a United Presbyterian Church of North America ship that plied the Nile River on missionary work. They stayed on board and spent days exploring a nearby garden. Amid the sunshine and blooming flowers, Biddy read the *Daily Light* and her beloved psalms. God spoke to her with a "supernatural intimacy" through the readings. He brought another message out of John 14:27: "Let not your heart be troubled, neither let it be afraid."[4]

One evening, as Biddy sat alone on deck praying, God reminded her of the last words she heard Oswald speak, echoing John 14:12: "Greater works than these shall he do; because I go unto my Father."

I felt as if God were there in Person by my side actually speaking the words to me, and instantly everything that had seemed to shut one in to the immediate present, lifted . . . assurance came, dimly at first, of a work yet to be done for Him.[5]

Biddy watched the endless river flow, prayed, and contemplated William Jessop's request. Perhaps she remembered one of Oswald's last talks, based on Ecclesiastes 9, where he said:

The Bible never allows us to waste time over the departed. It does not mean that the fact of human grief is ignored, but the worship of reminiscence is never allowed . . . [The] opportunity is lost forever; you cannot alter it, but arise and go to the next thing. . . . A man has to "ring out the grief that saps the mind."[6]

Oswald's words recognized the importance of mourning, but Kathleen needed her mother and the work at Zeitoun must continue. As Biddy later explained, while God had released Oswald from his tasks, he had not released her. The ministry at Zeitoun might not be as "radiant" as when under Oswald's guidance, but with God's direction it could still be fruitful.

Her husband had already prepared Biddy for the eventuality of his not being at Zeitoun. As she wrote:

When it was decided that my husband should go up to Palestine with the men, which meant we had to face carrying on the work without him, the word God spoke was—"As I was with Moses, so will I be with thee. I will not fail thee, nor forsake thee . . . Only be strong and very courageous" (Josh. 1:5).

I wrote the promise down, together with others, and it was a wonderful experience to re-read the words later and realize how much more God had meant in giving the promise than one had ever dreamt.[7]

Kathleen's matter-of-fact acceptance of Oswald's death encouraged her mother as well. "Don't forget, Daddy's quite near you," the little girl would declare, or, "Isn't it lovely, Daddy's with Jesus?" Her confidence in God awed and steadied Biddy.

The Zwemers' daughter, Bessie, came to see Biddy one evening. Oswald had nicknamed her "Bulger" when she joined him to play the piano on those Wednesday nights at Ezbekieh Gardens. The eighteen-year-old woman struggled with her faith during the war years and had sought counsel from Oswald.

Devastated at his death, Bessie sat with Biddy on the *Ibis* deck in the lengthening dusk and described Oswald's importance to her spiritual life. Pausing to glance around, she gasped.

Biddy followed her gaze to a nearby table. "What is it?"

The young woman's eyes grew wide. "Oswald was sitting right there. He said I shouldn't be troubled. I can't understand God's ways, but I need to focus on love."

Biddy nodded. While she hadn't seen anything, she did not discount Bessie's vision.[8]

Dr. and Mrs. Phillips provided a sanctuary. Later in the week, they escorted Biddy, Eva, and Kathleen to see the Luxor tourist sites. The party returned in time to watch the sun set over the Valley of the Kings on the Nile's western bank. Life and death, visions and dreams, often folded over themselves in ancient Luxor.

Meanwhile, Miss Riley and Gladys carried on at Zeitoun.

On November 17, the night after Oswald's burial and Biddy's departure, Jessop and his secretaries arranged for a memorial service. A thousand people crammed into the main hut to honor the "O. C., the Officer in Charge," Oswald Chambers.

At Biddy's request, Gladys sang "Jesus Triumphant" and described Oswald's years at the Bible Training College. George Swan recounted Oswald's ministry and love for his family. Numerous soldiers spoke of Oswald's influence on their lives. Stanley Barling of the YMCA described the service as one of "glad triumph and thanksgiving for the life that had been taken. . . . Through the singing of the hymn 'God is our refuge and our strength,' the realization came afresh . . . that God was with us yet."[9] Sidrak Effendi, the native handyman who worked on the Zeitoun building projects, talked of Oswald's good teaching and his gentleness with the Egyptian servants. Mourners were reluctant to leave when the service ended.

Several days later, Jimmy Hanson returned from England (without his bride, who still awaited permission to travel). The news of Oswald's death shocked him. While Jessop trusted Biddy's capabilities, he asked Jimmy to stay on to provide the leadership of a YMCA secretary on the premises. They needed him more at Zeitoun than at the front lines. Jimmy agreed in principle, but wanted to discuss the idea with Biddy.

After a week in Luxor, Biddy, Eva, and Kathleen journeyed north to Wasta, sixty miles south of Cairo on the Nile River. There they met Bessie Zwemer's friends Mr. and Mrs. Wilkinson. The Wilkinsons lived on the west bank of the Nile, where Mr. Wilkinson ran the pumping station. Cut off from society by the wide river, their home "Korimat" basked in a lush estate of blooming flowers, vegetables, and fruit trees. Bessie had provided them with copies of Oswald's sermons and the Wilkinsons wanted to hear more about God from Biddy.

Jimmy traveled down on November 23, and marveled afterward about Biddy's composure.

> One's first thoughts for her to whom he had meant everything were of deep sympathy and prayer. These were needed, but also one had to offer praise to God to see the marvelous calm and quiet fortitude, no rebellion, no questioning, but a real living testimony of Christ's own words, "Believe also on Me," and also of the words and teaching of our beloved Principal.[10]

Learning that Jimmy would be assigned to Zeitoun relieved Biddy of some of her concerns. He would take charge of the camp administration; she would teach a class on biblical psychology, using Oswald's book as a textbook.

After all the times she had heard Oswald speak on the subject and all the notes she had taken, not to mention putting together his book, Biddy did not worry about leading classes. Sharing the reading and discussion with the soldiers might make it easier for everyone. She also agreed to teach a series of studies on St. John's Gospel.

Given opportunity to reflect and ponder, Biddy began to make sense of the way "God began to interpret the sorrow in the light of His unfailing goodness and love."[11] They remained at Korimat for a week, finally returning to Zeitoun on November 30.

As they stood in the entrance to the camp upon their arrival, Biddy observed the groups of men clustered around the huts and people gathering for suppertime fellowship and prayers. Mary Riley and her helpers bustled with food preparations. Kathleen yearned to greet her menagerie.

Everything looked the same.

Everything was utterly different.

Biddy took a deep breath and recalled the morning's readings from the *Daily Light*: "My presence shall go with thee," and "Jesus Himself came and stood in the midst of them."[12]

Those words expressed what God had been to Biddy. She straightened her shoulders and walked past Oswald's YMCA sign into camp. Even without her husband's physical presence, his example of ministry propelled Biddy into the future.

Hobbs family, circa 1901. Standing center: Herbert Hobbs, standing right: Edith "Dais" Hobbs, seated center: Emily Hobbs. Biddy front left, Marian Leman front right. Other two unknown.

Biddy's sister, "Dais," circa 1898.

Oswald Chambers the year Biddy first met him, 1906.

Edward and Marian Leman Moore, 1909.

Chambers wedding party, May 25, 1910. Standing, left to right: best man Percy Lockhart, Dais Hobbs; Oswald's sister Gertrude, Herbert Hobbs. Seated: Oswald and Biddy, with his niece, Doris, in front.

League of Prayer, circa 1911. Sitting, left to right: Biddy, unknown, Mrs. Reader Harris (widow of Reader Harris), Mrs. Mary Hooker (daughter of Reader Harris), unknown. Standing, left to right: Miss Briscoe, unknown, unknown, unknown, unknown, unknown. Men standing left to right: Rev. David Lambert, James Gardiner, Rees Thomas, Oswald, unknown.

#45 Clapham Common North Side. Bible Training College.

Biddy and Oswald in BTC garden,
circa 1911.

Mary Riley, circa 1911.

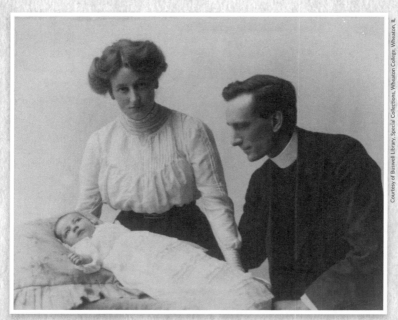

Biddy, Oswald, and baby Kathleen, summer 1913.

BTC student body, 1914. Row 1: unknown, Gladys Ingram, unknown, Muriel Bailey, unknown, Eva Spink, unknown.

Row 2: Mary Tweddle, Dorothea Reader Harris, unknown, Biddy, Oswald & Kathleen, Mrs. Reader Harris, Howard Hooker, Mrs. Mary Hooker, Katherine Ashe, unknown.

Row 3: unknown, Mary Riley, unknown, Miss M.E. Lawson, unknown, Miss Rosa Gardner, unknown, unknown, Miss Ann Blakeman, George Smith, unknown.

Row 4: unknown, unknown, Violet Richardson, unknown, Flo Gudgin, Mable Dempster, unknown, unknown.

Norah and Charles Rae Griffin, circa 1917.

Miss Katherine Ashe on the Askrigg moors, circa 1915.

Holiday in Askrigg, 1915. Standing: Arthur Chambers, Biddy, Oswald, Eva Spink, Jim Skidmore, Jimmy Hanson. Middle row: Gertrude Chambers, Bertha Chambers, Kathleen, Mary Riley. Front: Gladys Ingram, Flo Gudgin, Clare Warren (possibly).

Oswald in YMCA uniform, fall 1915.

BTC, 1915. Oswald, Biddy, and Kathleen.

Zeitoun compound, March 1916. Jimmy Hanson, Miss Ashe, Mary Riley, Philip Hancock, Biddy, Oswald, Kathleen, Effendi Sidrak.

The bungalow, Zeitoun, March 1916. Oswald seated left, Biddy and Mary Riley seated right. Miss Ashe standing in door. Jimmy Hanson seated far right.

Marquee main tent, Zeitoun, March 1916. From left: Philip Hancock, Jimmy Hanson, Oswald, Mary Riley, Biddy with Kathleen, Miss Ashe.

Swan family with Kathleen (far left), circa 1918. Mrs. Dora Swan, Barbara, Martin, Douglas, John David, and baby Hugh Christopher.

Zeitoun: taken from second floor of Egypt General Mission home. Left to right: study hut, devotional hut, and the bungalow, with bell tent in front.

Zeitoun, main YMCA hut, circa 1917.

Interior, YMCA main hut at Zeitoun, circa 1917.

Interior of devotional hut when Oswald taught a small group.

Oswald at Zeitoun YMCA compound main entrance, circa 1917.

They made Zeitoun beautiful.

Kathleen at Zeitoun, circa 1916.

Eva Spink.

Private Stephen Pulford, Zeitoun.

Final photo of Oswald, fall 1917.

Oswald and Biddy, summer 1917; final photo of couple together.

Oswald's burial cortege, November 16, 1917.

Oswald's burial service, Old Cairo Cemetery, November 16, 1917.

One hundred military officers marched behind Oswald's funeral caisson, November 16, 1917.

Oswald Chambers grave, Old Cairo cemetery, circa 1918.

Biddy and Kathleen, Oxford, circa 1921.

Biddy, Kathleen, and unknown friend,
Oxford, circa 1923.

Philip and Gertrude Kathleen Hancock
with daughter Mary, circa 1925.

Vyvyan and Gladys Ingram Donnithorne with daughter Audrey, circa 1925.

Biddy and Kathleen, Oxford, circa 1927.

Biddy, circa 1938.

# 12

## The Fires of Sorrow

### *1918*

The way to find yourself is in the fires of sorrow.[1]

*B*iddy picked up her notebook and pencil and walked down the stone-lined path—the stones whitewashed by Oswald himself—to the devotion hut.

She paused outside the mat door, listening to the murmur of deep voices inside. Slivers of light shone through the matting and cast a pattern onto the night-darkened sand.

At 7:30, Biddy tugged open the lightweight door and stepped inside. Her eyes automatically went to the front of the packed room and she felt a pang. No tall, lanky man smiled at her with an encouraging nod; she had no reason to slip into the back row this night.

Instead, the voices hushed and the whole roomful of soldiers watched her. Perhaps one man stood to say, "Welcome back, Mrs. Chambers. We're very sorry about your loss."

She gazed at the determined faces. These men knew the jolting grief of an unexpected death and were preparing themselves for the possibility of their own life ending too soon. Here were people who understood, far better than others, what she felt.

"Thank you." Biddy pressed a reassuring smile onto her lips and threaded her way to the front. She set down her notebook on the small table and turned to the blackboard, chalked that afternoon with an outline of the night's discussion.

In a calm, clear voice, she prayed a simple prayer and then picked up a copy of *Biblical Psychology*, Oswald's first book, published by the editors of *God's Revivalist and Bible Advocate* magazine.

"Oswald is not here to teach us and so we will learn together now," she said. Opening the book, Biddy read Oswald's preface and then launched into the first chapter, "Man: His Creation, Calling and Communion."

Biddy still rose early every morning but no longer had her husband beside her. She watched the sunrise, drank her tea, read the *Daily Light*, and prayed alone, mapping out the busy day in her mind. Lamentations 3 helped: "This I recall to my mind, therefore have I hope. It is of the LORD's mercies that we are not consumed, because his compassions fail not. They are new every morning: great is thy faithfulness" (vv. 21–23).

God's faithfulness could be seen in the smooth transition as Biddy and Kathleen were surrounded by BTC friends at the Zeitoun camp. The people who loved them were wise, and they focused on God's glory in the difficult circumstances. As Biddy wrote to friends in England:

Unbelief said "What can we do?" But faith said "What cannot God do?"

In this confidence, we stepped out into the new thing God had for us, and bit by bit God revealed His mind about the different parts of the work and so wonderfully gave us the wisdom we sought. Now I do feel that God's order for this place is being fulfilled.[2]

The soldiers continued to come. Just as Biddy and Jimmy planned, two nights a week they studied *Biblical Psychology* together and one evening Biddy led them through the Gospel of John. Army "padres" (chaplains) took services on the other nights.

Biddy oversaw a League of Prayer–style meeting on Saturday nights. The black prayer notebook from this time includes long lists of soldiers' names, many serving at the front.

Sundays remained full. Biddy took the morning service every other week, with her BTC colleagues filling in the rest of the time. Free teas still drew hundreds of men. More than one soldier told the canteen workers how long it had been to the date since he last took tea in such a civilized manner.

A chaplain led the Sunday evening service and served communion once a month. Afterward, Biddy and friends gathered for supper and a hymn, usually "The Day Thou Gavest, Lord, Is Ended," followed by prayer. They still walked together into the desert night to admire the stars.

No one forgot Oswald. The matron at Aotea Home wrote, "We feel absolutely lost on Sunday mornings now, his talks have been a tremendous help to many of our men and also to the numbers of the staff. . . . He has left a blank at Aotea that cannot be filled."[3] Biddy often heard similar sentiments as men and women struggled to understand the *why* of Oswald's death.

Grateful for her two weeks to mourn, Biddy knew she must set a tone of calm for the others. One friend marveled at how Biddy set aside her own sorrow to console others. Eva never spoke of her two weeks mourning with Biddy other than to express a deep thanksgiving for being there. Biddy, for her part, wrote Eva's parents, telling them how much Eva's brave spirit and never-wavering faith had meant to her at Wasta.

Biddy received countless letters from soldiers, YMCA secretaries, and missionaries in the first weeks after her return to Zeitoun. While they'd sent the news immediately to England—and the League of

Prayer held a memorial service in Caxton Hall on December 5—the condolence letters took time to travel overseas.

She wanted to respond to the sympathy letters in a God-affirming way, and Jimmy suggested an idea. He had saved copies of Oswald's talks printed in the League of Prayer's *Tongues of Fire* magazine. He showed the scrapbook to Biddy and suggested printing an excerpt from a talk titled "The Place of Help."

Based on Psalm 121, the 1,800-word pamphlet reminded readers "not to the great things God has done, not to the noble saints and noble lives He has made, but to God Himself does the Psalmist point." It wasn't simply an excellent lesson for men slogging through a war. The pamphlet also reminded readers, "We have not been told to follow in all the footsteps of the mountain-like characters, but in the footsteps of their faith, because their faith is in a Person." For people grieving over Oswald Chambers's death, the pamphlet pointed them to the God he worshiped—just as Oswald always insisted.[4]

More letters of appreciation arrived, and the next month Biddy printed another talk, "Building for Eternity." The positive response encouraged Biddy to arrange to print one of Oswald's talks into a pamphlet each month.

By this time, Nile Mission Press in Cairo had published *Baffled to Fight Better* and she gave away free copies of the book. Samuel Zwemer liked it so much he ordered one hundred copies to share with his fellow missionaries. Biddy mailed a dozen copies to her family and eighty-eight to the League of Prayer in England.

Christmas came, and while Biddy and Kathleen stayed home, Jimmy, Eva, Gladys, and Miss Riley traveled into Cairo to visit Oswald's grave. There they thanked God for their beloved teacher and how his words had led them to a deeper walk with Jesus.

Meanwhile, the pamphlets were in demand at all sixty YMCA centers in war theaters. Biddy often had only a few left to send home for distribution among readers of her circular letters and Oswald's diary excerpts. She finally sent a copy of each pamphlet to Gertrude Chambers and suggested she arrange to have them reprinted and distributed in England.

Gertrude turned to the usual reliable source for publishing help. Charles Rae Griffin, now returned, injured, from the war, gathered a group of friends and opened a fund for publishing costs. They made arrangements to republish *Baffled to Fight Better* and the other pamphlets. Oswald used to talk about God engineering their circumstances, and that it was important to remember God's ways often seemed haphazard to the human mind.⁵ Even in his grief, Griffin saw the possibilities of Biddy's notes providing quality biblical teaching.

Biddy received one hundred letters one January 1918 day, including, at last, a letter from her family written after Oswald's death. While that letter does not survive, Biddy's response does—full of simple news and her desire to sit and talk with her mother and Dais.

The only personal comment beyond the wish to see her family was Biddy's description of Kathleen's response to hearing Dais and Emily's letter read aloud. "Oh, I do want to go home and see them!"⁶ The little girl had no memory of England, her aunt, or her grandmother. Biddy had to wonder how long Kathleen would remember Oswald.

Both Biddy and her mother had lost their fathers as teenagers. Emily Hobbs craved financial security the rest of her life as a result. Biddy used her grief from Henry Hobbs's death to focus on being able to provide for herself as a stenographer. They both remembered their fathers well. But would Kathleen?

An insightful four and a half years old, Kathleen already knew how to read.⁷ In the familiar Zeitoun compound surrounded by people who loved Kathleen and her parents, the little girl was reminded of Oswald daily. Biddy spoke of him naturally, always remembering his advice to pay close attention to Kathleen and not rely on sympathetic others to tend her.

Kathleen processed her father's death in her own way, ministering to everyone in the camp with her matter-of-fact faith. Gladys described Kathleen's natural and joyful simplicity while playing with her toys and casually discussing with the soldiers what her daddy was doing in heaven.

It was all very real to Kathleen. She asked her mother in January, "You must think Daddy is much safer up in heaven?"[8] How could Biddy answer that? A widow with children acutely knows the value of her own life. If a child has only one parent, losing the second would make her an orphan.

Biddy believed God had reasons for giving her Kathleen to raise without a father. God also had provided a task: to put Oswald's teachings into writing for the spiritual benefit of others. She believed God would care for her and her child as she performed her ministry.

But the stresses on Biddy's life mounted. She had spent fall 1917 preparing for Oswald's planned departure to the front lines coupled with assuming responsibility for the work at Zeitoun. Oswald's shocking illness and death sapped her energy and emotions—including her desire to be a good example for others. Before she found her equanimity, the long-anticipated battle for Jerusalem erupted with severe casualties as the deadly war inched closer to Cairo and its hospitals. Even happy events like Christmas and visits by dear friends brought their own stresses, not to mention the overwhelming number of sympathy letters needing a reply.

She was, simply, a very new widow with a young child far from home in a war zone.

Modern psychologists believe once stress, even good stress, reaches a certain level, an individual becomes susceptible to illness. Given all she had been through, it's not surprising Biddy succumbed to influenza followed by jaundice in early February 1918.

Jaundice epidemics occurred periodically among the troops in Egypt during WWI. (The Canadian Forces Medical Service traced its infectiousness to rats on the battlefield.)[9] Up to 25 percent of

ANZAC troops fell ill with jaundice, particularly those stationed near Alexandria.

Jaundice symptoms included headache, loss of appetite, ache over the stomach, and a yellowish hue spreading over the skin or around the whites of the eyes. Biddy couldn't think clearly, caught in a "brain fog."[10] Once again, YMCA friends packed her up and sent her back to Korimat, this time with Kathleen and Miss Riley in attendance. Both women needed rest.

Dr. and Mrs. Phillips readily opened their beautiful home. Jaundice generally lasted from one to six weeks and required bed rest until the aching tiredness diminished, along with the yellowish skin tone. Kathleen diligently checked her mother's fading yellow coloring each morning while Biddy spent a month recuperating.

Once again, she watched the Nile River flow by as she prayed, read, wrote letters, thought, and napped. Her relative proximity to Zeitoun meant friends visited and delivered mail. Biddy appreciated hearing that Emily and Dais understood why she remained in a war zone with a preschool child far from home. In responding, Biddy acknowledged their challenges in dealing with rationing (residents of the British Isles hadn't seen a banana since 1914, for example). Biddy didn't worry about food; compared to England, Egypt was a land of plenty.

Dr. and Mrs. Phillips had read Oswald's book and pamphlets now and recognized what a difference understanding God's truth made in their lives. Biddy wrote about their response to her mother and sister:

> It confirms me so much in the assurance I have that I am to go on getting everything I can printed. It will be like casting bread upon the waters and we'll know someday all it has meant in people's lives. I am more and more grateful to have the work to do. I feel like John that the world couldn't contain the writings if I were to get all my notes printed.[11]

During one conversation, Mrs. Phillips echoed a familiar warning. She saw Kathleen as God's messenger to Biddy, and reminded her no one else could bring Kathleen up for God. Biddy must be faithful in her mothering.[12]

Kathleen Ballinger and Gladys visited, taking turns "spelling" Miss Riley so she could see to affairs at Zeitoun. The two young women blessed Biddy with their presence but also savored time to rest themselves. Eighteen months after their arrival in Egypt, they showed physical strain and exhaustion from the never-ending labor and difficult conditions. Eventually even Miss Ashe and Eva visited Korimat, a place they all recognized as a perfect gift from God.[13]

Biddy returned to camp in March, healthy and with a renewed sense of the value of her transcription and publication work. As news of Oswald's free pamphlets spread, requests poured in. By the beginning of summer, the Nile Mission Press printed thousands of copies a month for Biddy to distribute.

William Jessop watched all this, understanding well the importance of Biddy's work in continuing Oswald's ministry. In early summer, he approached Biddy and volunteered to have the YMCA take over responsibility for printing and distributing the pamphlets among YMCA centers across the war theater—which included Europe. She only needed to provide the text. She agreed, and Nile Mission Press would produce ten thousand pamphlets a month for YMCA distribution until July 1919.

As Jessop explained in his annual report, "Mr. Chambers has gone to the Father but his work still goes on, for Mrs. Chambers is publishing his sermons and talks as leaflets for distribution among the troops and they are exerting a wide influence in spiritual up building."[14]

During summer 1918, the ministry in Benha ended and Miss Ashe moved to Jerusalem to help run a YMCA hostel. Kathleen Ballinger shifted to Zeitoun to complete her wedding plans. When the time came, little Kathleen served as the bridesmaid in a white dress, carrying a bouquet of flowers to match the radiant bride. The new Mr. and Mrs. Philip Hancock honeymooned in Wasta and then took up residence in Ismailia to minister to the troops stationed nearby.

Her growing daughter reminded Biddy of her father, and she blessed God for the joy of mothering her, even in their unconventional life. They visited the zoo together, and Biddy loved to hear her daughter praying about "fundamental things."[15]

The Egyptian summer sizzled—often 105 degrees in the shade—but at Zeitoun Biddy typed and did paperwork in the relative cool of Oswald's dugout. She and Kathleen spent a few days near the seashore for a breath of refreshing air.

War news continued to be brutal as the German army tried to conquer faraway France before the American army could arrive in full force. The ANZAC troops drilled and prepared to ship out to Europe, and old friends came and went through the School of Instruction.

Tea and late-night suppers were full of friendly faces telling stories, singing, and praying together. Biddy enjoyed leading the discussion groups and her own meetings. She never had time to mope or feel abandoned, since many sought her out to talk about Oswald. They thanked her for keeping his teachings alive.

When the armistice finally came on November 11, 1918, Biddy rejoiced with the rest of the world. She noted in her diary, "It's too much to grasp all at once, but one's heart is full of praise now; it will be wonderful to voice."[16]

November 15 dawned a glorious morning, just as Oswald had described so often. Stephen Pulford visited and gave Kathleen a new doll, but the gift did not stop her from commenting to her mother, "I never forget Daddy because his home is in my heart."[17] They traveled to the cemetery and left flowers.

Before he departed for home in Australia, Peter Kay arranged for a stone Bible carved with Luke 11:13 to be laid on the grave.

(The verse echoed the banner Oswald had posted above the Zeitoun hut platform. In 2016, however, only a traditional WWI memorial headstone marked Oswald's grave.)[18]

In late 1918, Gladys and Eva applied for return permits to England. Theo Atkinson sailed for England, while ANZAC friends repatriated to Australia and New Zealand. Even Mrs. Jessop departed home to America—before she left, she requested copies of all Oswald's sermons to be reprinted by the American YMCA National Council.

Biddy's friends worked to make Christmas 1918 happy. Five-and-a-half-year-old Kathleen rejoiced in her pile of gifts; they decorated the large hut with a Christmas tree sent from Wasta. Jimmy Hanson's grin grew wide at the news that his bride, Flo, would finally join him at Zeitoun. But a stiff-upper-lip sadness filled Biddy's heart when Eva and Gladys sailed home from Port Said in early January 1919.

While the armistice had ceased hostilities, it still took many months for troops to be returned to their home countries. The YMCA still served the armed forces in a variety of ways—including sorting and helping POWs. At Zeitoun, ministry continued at a decreased tempo and Biddy remained at her oversight post with Jimmy Hanson.

Life progressed as in the past. She visited the pyramids and the Sphinx on a donkey, entertained friends, transcribed, prepared pamphlets, and taught classes. Biddy developed a calendar of Oswald's sayings and spent long days typing in the dugout.

Printed by the Nile Mission Press in early 1919, the first *Seed Thoughts Calendar* collected the daily thoughts Oswald had written on the study hut blackboard. They included pithy statements like the one for January 22: "The resentment of discipline of any kind will warp the whole life away from God's purpose."[19]

Biddy designed the simple booklet to be narrow and thin, easy to fit into the breast pocket of a soldier's uniform. She placed copies on the Sunday night free literature table and they promptly disappeared. Soldiers requested more copies to share with others in their tents or to send home to their families.

Biddy's sense of God's direction and guidance in preparing the pamphlets brought her great satisfaction. Each finished project encouraged her, and the letters of thanks and requests for more from all over the world reinforced the works' value. Biddy rejoiced when she thought of how many notebooks full of shorthand notes from the BTC days waited in stored trunks in London. She foresaw no end to the books she could produce and began work on the next one, *Shadow of an Agony.*

Meanwhile, the fellowship that sustained her dwindled. Miss Riley remained steadfast and Miss Ashe visited between YMCA station assignments. The Swan family still resided at the EGM house, though some of the children could now go to England for boarding school. The fulfilling days of Zeitoun were slowing, though tasks for Biddy persisted.

In April, Biddy wrote long letters to Eva and her swain, Stephen "Tim" Pulford, discussing their relationship with God and each other. Eva apparently was debating breaking off the relationship because of Tim's lack of faith. Biddy wrote to her, "I personally believe that the crisis will prove to Tim that He is 'there' in simple confidence God, and that he'll come out . . . as a disciple and, as you say, for that we can watch with Him. Perhaps it had to come to this way that the love as God designed it might emerge clear and pure." She included various Bible passages to back up her thoughts.[20]

To Tim, on the same day, Biddy wrote, "I believe these days are going to mean a lot in your lives and I am sure your attitude of simple trust in God is the one to have and one which will enable God to reveal Himself to you. . . . I believe you'd find you have a lot in common with Job as Oswald wrote in *Baffled to Fight Better.*"[21]

Biddy's letters often included references to things Oswald had said in the past or through his books. Full of love and encouragement, her letters centered on the things of God first—with biblical truth as her lens. Her scrawl could be challenging to read but the letters were always positive and full of hope. Writing letters—often multiple pages long—kept Biddy busy; she always ended them, "Lovingly, Biddy."

The School of Instruction's closure marked the end of the ANZAC camp at Zeitoun. In April 1919, with the soldiers all gone and while they awaited permits to sail for England, Biddy and Kathleen took a trip to Jerusalem to see where Jesus had walked.

Nearly six, Kathleen proved an excellent traveling companion as they toured the traditional sites: the Dome on the Rock, the Wailing Wall, the Garden of Gethsemane, and even Bethlehem. Kathleen dipped her toes into the Pool of Siloam and declared herself "healed," though on the final trip—to see Abraham, Sarah, Isaac, and Rebecca's tomb—the little girl refused to visit yet another grave.

The landscape leading up to Jerusalem remained scarred from army efforts to take the city in December 1917. War's tortured battlefield debris reminded Biddy of the men they had spiritually prepared for the battles. Reflecting on the horrors, Biddy marveled anyone had survived, much less fought on to free Jerusalem from the Ottoman Empire.[22]

They returned to Zeitoun to discover Kathleen and Philip Hancock had departed for England. Empty Zeitoun felt forsaken. Egypt saw rioting in the city streets that May, along with uprisings in distant corners of the nation. As soon as their permits to travel came through from the British authorities, the YMCA made arrangements to close up camp. Finally, Biddy could go home.

The day before Biddy, Kathleen, Mary, and Jimmy and Flo Hanson departed, they took one last trip to the Old Cairo cemetery. There they left flowers on a place, Biddy wrote, "From which one is never far in spirit . . . we thanked God for all the knowledge of Himself that had come to us during the years in Egypt."[23]

With her daughter in hand, Biddy Chambers stepped onto a ship and faced the reality of a radically new life in England.

# 13

## Sublime Intimacy

### *1919–20*

Faith . . . can be turned into a personal possession only through conflict.[1]

*T*he war may have been over and the Versailles Treaty signed in June 1919, but the world remained in upheaval as nations sorted themselves into new borders. The Spanish flu pandemic was at its height (ultimately killing twenty million people) and years of deprivation left citizens anxious and in no mood to compromise.

Hostilities did not cease with the treaty; many simply went underground as people turned against each other. Imperial Russia collapsed under the Bolshevik revolution, Germany's populace struggled to eat, and England's workers went on strike. France's battlefields are still being cleared of live ordnance to this day; likewise, lead-contaminated fish in the Somme River remain unsafe to eat.

Demobilization and transport home for civilians from the war theaters proceeded in a disorganized fashion; travelers took whatever berths they could find. We don't know the name of the ship on which Biddy's party sailed in late June 1919, though it may have been one of the steamships recently returned to mail service between England and Australia.

They left the sunny skies of Port Said and sailed across the Mediterranean Sea through warm, balmy days without fear of U-boats. Their ship could sail through the Straits of Gibraltar in daylight, and the major shipping lanes were clear of known mines. Mesmerized by the ocean, Biddy watched from a deck chair when her daughter didn't require attention. She spent her time praying and contemplating what the future held for her truncated family of two.

Biddy had traveled to Egypt three and a half years before, following Oswald's lead into a ministry given by God. With Oswald and dreams for a post-war Bible school dead, Biddy needed to create her own life in an England roiled by societal changes. She carried in her heart a charge to produce Oswald's dictated material into readable form. The way seemed open, the demand called, her skills provided, and a trunk full of BTC notebooks beckoned. Charles Griffin and others waited for her and "the books" she would create.

She breathed the moisture-laden salty air and relaxed. Hadn't God always provided for them? When Jimmy Hanson chased the sprightly Kathleen past her, Biddy laughed. God always sent friends to lighten her tasks when she needed them.

The last five members of the BTC Expeditionary Force landed at Southampton on Thursday, July 3, 1919, and caught the boat train to London's Waterloo station. The League of Prayer's *Spiritual Life* magazine announced their return in the next edition, noting "they all looked fine and well with a touch of the real Eastern complexion, while Kathleen has grown from a kiddie in arms to a little slip of a girl, all sun-bonnet and smiles, and so like her daddy."[2]

Finally, Biddy got to hug her sister Dais and mother Emily. Finally, they could sit down over a cup of tea for a long chat. Finally, Kathleen could kiss and hug the two women who had sustained the family with packages as long as the little girl could remember. Finally, they were home.

Except England didn't feel like home.

For a little girl used to living outdoors with a menagerie, the bustle of an Army camp, and the singsong of native voices, London was a foreign place. Dais and Emily Hobbs's rooms stuffed with furniture, books, and hushed voices didn't contain space for a rambunctious girl used to the doting attention of boisterous soldiers. The humidity in the air, the rattle of passing motor vehicles, the smell of gas rings instead of outdoor cooking fires, all meant adjustments for Kathleen and probably for Biddy as well.

London felt tense and controlled. The city and people looked worn, the sky overcast, the views cramped. Kathleen missed Zeitoun's freedoms, wide blue sky, and stunning sunsets.

Dais and Emily could provide a cramped home and food, nothing more. It fell to Biddy to raise her daughter in the new old world. Unlike the conspicuous war widows clad in black, Biddy had no pension and few financial resources. But she had confidence in God and his promises, as she wrote in her diary: "It is a joy to step out in complete dependence in God and to look forward to the new things He will open up."[3]

In the first weeks, she welcomed visitors delighted to see her and to marvel at how much Kathleen had grown. They all wanted to hear accounts of Oswald's death and their life in Egypt. Well-intentioned friends asked the logical question: "What will you do next?"

Prepare more Oswald teachings for publication.

Everyone loved the idea, even if they didn't quite understand the work involved. Friends and League of Prayer members donated funds to defray costs, thrilled Oswald's lessons would continue, even without him.

Mrs. Howard Hooker soon sent over the trunks long stored in her basement. Biddy knelt beside the one housing her notes, unlocked it, and lifted the lid.

Stacks of notebooks filled the trunk, their covers labeled with the titles of the talks and the dates she wrote them. Shorthanded squiggles mixed with standard cursive spread before Biddy, recalling her to the back row of the opulent BTC classroom or the utilitarian League of Prayer meeting halls. Biddy flipped through a notebook, effortlessly reading symbols that looked like hieroglyphics to Dais and Emily.

Here was Oswald's legacy: notebooks stacked and tied with ribbon. "The Discipline of Loneliness" lecture included a quote from Tennyson that sang in her memory. Tears blurred Biddy's eyes. She could once again feel the firm desktop under her notebook, smell the shavings from her pencil, and hear Oswald's voice speaking the verses. Her chest constricted. He was gone. She'd never hear her husband speak again, but his words and thoughts lived.

The memories flooded—all those discussions, Oswald speaking and Biddy taking it down. Did the idea of turning his ideas into books still thrill her? She smoothed her hand down a page and examined the marks. She whispered aloud as she read and, when Kathleen joined her, Biddy pointed to the shorthand. "These are your daddy's words."

"Can you turn these notes into books?" Dais asked.

"Yes," Biddy said. "I want to."

Elated by how much material she had to work with, Biddy blew the Egyptian sand from her boxy typewriter and began revising the *Seed Thoughts Calendar*. This type of ancillary product appealed to busy readers: short quotes printed for each day of the year on a calendar, 366 quotes in all. It would not be expensive to produce or sell during England's tight financial times.

Biddy combed through the notebooks, perhaps looking for re-membered statements, maybe choosing what made the most sense for a specific day like Christmas or Easter. The Cairo YMCA had published the last pamphlet in July 1919; she wanted to continue placing her husband's words and thoughts into the religious liter-ary market as soon as possible.

Still looking after her frail parents at 11 Tintagle Crescent in Dulwich, forty-seven-year-old Gertrude Chambers urged Biddy on and offered to help. Gertrude had never stopped receiving and often answering mail on Biddy and Oswald's behalf. She regularly sent off requested copies of Oswald's *Baffled to Fight Better* and other pamphlets. Biddy happily left the mail to Gertrude.

Meanwhile, Biddy's typing and Kathleen's energy soon proved too much for the nearly seventy-year-old Emily Hobbs's nerves. Biddy recognized they could not stay comfortably with her family and so, when BTC friends Eric and Gladys Ofvenberg offered a room in their apartment near Finsbury Park, she moved in early September.

The Ofvenbergs, their three-year-old, Kathleen, and Biddy shared the modest apartment and living expenses for the next eighteen months. Eric worked for Westminster Bank. Biddy contributed to the household through donations of food and money from family and friends.

In this new location, Kathleen could sing and dance without fear of breaking anything and Biddy could type. The Ofvenbergs happily participated in sharing Oswald's wisdom with friends and encouraged Biddy to consider the house hers as well as theirs. As Biddy wrote in her diary, "My prayer is that God will make of this house as one of His open houses for the universe."[4] One night a week, Biddy hosted a class much like the one she led in the Zeitoun study hut after Oswald's death. The small group read through and discussed *Biblical Psychology*.

This group formed the core of those who helped Biddy. They included BTC regulars such as Charles and Norah Griffin. Dais, naturally, came each week. Mary Riley, with her fresh face and loyalty, traveled from the family home she shared with her father and sisters to attend. Gladys Ingram, busy organizing her wedding and making plans to move to China with Vyvyan Donnithorne, caught the Underground to the meetings, as did ever-enthusiastic Eva Spink. Former soldiers from the Zeitoun days included round-faced Stephen Pulford (who finally made his peace with God) and gap-toothed Louis Richard Samuel Clarke. Their continuing friendship and interest in studying Oswald's words warmed Biddy's heart, even as their monetary gifts for the books and to support her home life encouraged her.

Known for his publishing acumen and character, Charles Griffin recommended paper merchants, printers, and binders and oversaw Biddy's publishing arrangements (Charles Griffin & Company, Ltd. specialized in technical manuals and journals). Biddy had completed one-third of the revised *Seed Thoughts Calendar* when Griffin got her a September appointment with a publisher friend, Mr. Chamberlain.

Unfortunately, the interview didn't go well. When she outlined her projects and the nature of the already published material, Chamberlain saw no market or value in them. Biddy left feeling foolish. She could expect no help from his publishing house. Afterward, she described herself as feeling "undone" by the experience.

Biddy stood at a crossroads after meeting Chamberlain. The easiest way to publish Oswald's work would have been through a publisher. Publishing houses provided editors, publicity, and placement into bookstores. A publishing house would have paid Biddy an advance on future royalties to live on while she produced the manuscript. Once the published books had "earned back" the initial advance, Biddy would have received royalty payments as long as the books remained in print.[5] The risk of success or failure would fall to the publisher, not Biddy.

Despite Griffin's personal and professional enthusiasm, publishers in 1919 didn't understand the significance of Oswald's teachings nor recognize the potential for his work to sell. In trying to understand their rejection, perhaps Biddy remembered Oswald's reminder, "We are not called to success, but faithfulness."[6]

Not having a publisher made producing Oswald's books more difficult, but Biddy refused to be discouraged once she prayed about the meeting with Chamberlain. Instead, she chose to see the answer as a change of direction: "We must simply go on our way with God. It seemed like a closing of a chapter of the Y. M. work and that probably is just as it should be."

She ruefully added in her diary: "We're to use organizations without advising them—perhaps I was tempted to do the latter. I feel a clean space now, liberty only to go along the lines of spontaneous moral originality."[7]

Whether she understood or not, Biddy basically became a self-publisher ninety years before it was common. Within a week of her disheartening interview with Chamberlain, she completed the *Seed Thoughts Calendar*, laughing in her diary about her almost overwhelming desire to retype it! The project filled her heart with gladness—it contained so many wonderful thoughts, she could hardly wait to see it in print.

With the calendar completed, Biddy paged through her notebooks to decide on the next project. During this time the formidable Mrs. Reader Harris and her daughter Mrs. Howard Hooker visited. They brought a proposition for Biddy.

Mary Hooker had loved the Bible Training College and, with the end of the war, decided to open a similar school for women only. She had stored all the furniture since the BTC's closing and that summer moved it to a new Bible college called Ridgelands, located in Wimbledon, six miles southeast of Clapham Common. She wanted Biddy to run it with her.

Certainly the offer must have tempted Biddy. Ridgelands focused on the particular qualities and insights women brought to missionary work, especially in-depth Bible training.[8] Biddy's years at Zeitoun as a missionary and her superintendent role at the BTC well qualified her for the job. Running the school would mean a stipend and a home for Biddy and her child at a time when even war widows with one child received a paltry 21 shillings a month to live on (about US $50, 2014).[9]

The women genuinely liked each other and worked well together, but Biddy recalled Oswald's relief when Mrs. Harris severed the League's obligation to him in 1916. He had envisioned his own school after the war.

Running Ridgelands looked like an obvious solution to her situation, but it would demand her full attention, making it difficult to produce Oswald's books. Stephen Pulford would remember this time in Biddy's life. She was "destitute, living for many years below the bread line, yet in faith that God had called her to perpetuate her husband's message."[10]

Biddy took several days to pray and weigh the offer, but as she confided in her diary, "somehow I cannot feel the all over feeling that it is God's order,"[11] finally concluding that running a college was not her calling. Besides, as she explained to Mrs. Hooker and Mrs. Harris, she had a child to rear.

"We'll hire a nanny for Kathleen," Mrs. Harris said.

Her generosity brought clarity. How often had Biddy been reminded to care personally for Kathleen?

"No, thank you," Biddy replied. "Kathleen will be looked after by me."[12]

While she chose not to work at Ridgelands, Biddy honored her connection to the League of Prayer. The first few months home from Egypt, Biddy and Kathleen traveled to League of Prayer centers around Great Britain. Biddy spoke of Oswald's ministry and answered questions about his death, in addition to her standard talks on the psalms and the importance of Scripture memorization. League members had read about the YMCA ministry at Zeitoun in *Tongues of Fire* and wanted to hear more stories. Also, former soldiers from the YMCA hut in Egypt were eager to reconnect with her.

The round of reunions may have been pleasant for Biddy, but Kathleen was a restless child shuffled between lodgings and meeting strangers. At a stop near Liverpool, she succumbed to the measles, complicated by whooping cough. With a steaming teakettle and Biddy in attendance, Kathleen recuperated at the tiny home of faithful League of Prayer members. And then they continued on.

The speaking engagements took them to places she'd once visited with Oswald—and Biddy felt pangs of memory, despite the loving greetings of old friends. Grief may have tinged September 19 when she attended Gladys's wedding to Vyvyan Donnithorne with dear friends from her BTC and Zeitoun days. When the Donnithornes sailed to China a few months later as missionaries, Biddy wrote a wistful note in her diary: "It's difficult to realize she [Gladys] has really gone."[13]

Her close BTC friends were moving on with their post-war life, picking up the pieces or finding new possibilities.

Eva and Stephen Pulford married in 1920. Stephen attended the London College of Divinity and became an Anglican priest. Obviously, he had found God according to his own timetable.

Jimmy and Flo Hanson considered a return to YMCA work in Egypt but, following the birth of two sons in short order, decided to remain in England. They lived above a former music hall and ran a flourishing Methodist mission for the poor in London's notorious East End.

Philip and Kathleen Hancock voyaged to America in 1921 to attend a Presbyterian seminary near San Francisco, California. Miss Ashe remained in the Middle East, and Mary Riley lived with her family of dressmaking sisters.

As for Kathleen, Biddy enrolled her self-confident six-year-old in school that fall. In an uncharacteristic sentimental moment, Biddy wrote of this enormous transition as "the white funeral for her [Kathleen's] babyhood but she's growing finely as our flower of God."[14]

Suspicious of yet another new place, when she heard the news Kathleen pushed her doll's pram to school and demanded an interview with the principal. The school apparently passed Kathleen's muster and off she went, leaving Biddy with her notes and typewriter.

Biddy settled into the comfortable rhythm of London life, including a visit to the cinema to see General Allenby's pictures from Jerusalem—which made her homesick for the desert. She enjoyed classical concerts featuring music by Mendelssohn, Debussy, Wagner, and Tchaikovsky at Albert Hall. She and Kathleen visited the London Zoo with her sister-in-law Bee Hobbs and nephew Jack, where they saw Winnie, the Canadian bear who inspired A. A. Milne's book *Winnie the Pooh*.

But one day, when Kathleen came through the door, Biddy noticed her eating an apple. "Where did you get that?"

Kathleen shrugged. "I picked it up on the way home from school."

Biddy frowned at Oswald's Scallywag. "Where?"

The girl pointed out the window.

"At the greengrocer?" Biddy stared at her daughter.

"Like we always did at the canteen. I was hungry."

A mortified Biddy reached for her coin purse. Back in Zeitoun, Kathleen and David Swan had run all over the compound every day. When they waltzed through the canteen and were hungry, they would select a piece of fruit from the counter without anyone saying a word. No one taught the children otherwise.

She took Kathleen by the hand and walked her to the greengrocer. "Have you noticed my daughter taking fruit?"

He nodded.

Biddy sighed. "How much?"

Years later, Kathleen shook her head at this memory. "My mother had all sorts of bills to pay because I had to pass a greengrocer on the way to school."[15]

The first anniversary marking the end of World War I came on November 11, 1919, at eleven o'clock in the morning. King George V asked all Britons to stop their normal activities "so that in perfect stillness, the thoughts of every one may be concentrated on reverent remembrance of the glorious dead."[16] The "Great Silence" lasted two minutes. Motor vehicles idled, people halted, and the nation corporately remembered the dead. One observer noted the only sound heard was the rustle of leaves on the sidewalk.

Biddy and Dais attended services together that morning. She appreciated how the clergyman's prayers brought the presence of God into their midst. The two then went to lunch, took a walk in Regent's Park, and were home to welcome Kathleen when she returned from school.

Perhaps the hardest day was November 15, when Biddy went alone to St. Paul's Cathedral. In her diary she described it as a day of "God's gracious undertaking as I looked back over the two years so full of His almighty sufficiency."[17] God's presence felt very real to her in the cathedral, especially when the full organ played and she recalled her life-changing visit with Oswald in 1908.

From the cathedral Biddy traveled to Dulwich for tea with Oswald's parents and Gertrude. She enjoyed seeing them, particularly appreciating their prayer time together. The two years since Oswald's death had been full of hard work, ministry, uncertainty, and looking to God to supply her every need. In summing up the day, Biddy felt God had reminded her the joy of the Lord was her strength.

Biddy's diary ended in 1920. Her life was too busy to sustain it and book preparations took precedence over anything else. About this time, Biddy followed Griffin's counsel and arranged to publish her revised *Seed Thoughts Calendar*. After typing it to perfection, she turned it in for production to S. W. Partridge, Ltd., a printer and publisher of Christian books in London. The calendar/book appeared in 1921.

"Mrs. Chambers, left homeless, without means of support, and with a small daughter to educate, started absolutely from scratch," Stephen Pulford would remember. "Yet nothing daunted her in her enthusiasm to get her husband's message circulated. She would not take any funds from the books lest that cripple her ability to publish the next one."[18]

Some argued the financial "insurance" Oswald left were the notebooks filled with his words. In compiling and publishing the books and pamphlets with Oswald's name on the cover, Biddy might have earned an adequate living from the profit. But she did not see it that way.

"The money aspect was always so careful where my mother was concerned," Kathleen said. "We didn't spend the money or use the money except for putting the books in print. Nobody, as it were, sort of made anything out of the books except to have them continually in print."[19]

Producing the books was Biddy's offering to God. They provided the revenue for more books, and because Biddy didn't answer to a publisher on the numbers sold, she felt free to give away a book to whoever she thought needed one. Kathleen estimated her mother gave away seven to eight hundred books a year. Biddy's convictions about money and ministry may confound modern readers but made sense to her given Oswald's teaching. She insisted the words had been spoken to be distributed and that is why God honored what she did.[20]

Early in their marriage, Biddy and Oswald had agreed not to complain or talk about money issues. In early 1916, Oswald wrote in his diary:

Many have their intercourse with God rudely corrupted by the perpetual plaint of chronic impecuniousness. It is to my mind more of a shame to mention money in the way one so often hears than many other things considered more shameful.[21]

Biddy carried on in like manner through her widowhood, even as she lived in poverty. "I don't mean to say that God left us in the lurch," Kathleen said, "but we did go through very difficult times where money was concerned."[22]

The concept of God providing for needs—not necessarily wants— had been practiced by many nineteenth-century missionaries. George Mueller's orphanage and life demonstrated the spiritual concept of waiting on God's provision without mentioning the need to others. Oswald, of course, lived the same way.

Even if Biddy had been willing to seek employment beyond producing the books, jobs were difficult to find for women following the war. Returning servicemen claimed available positions, causing the percentage of women workers to decline after the war. In addition, the British economy spiraled into a recession, triggering high levels of unemployment almost as soon as hostilities concluded. Women workers were editorialized in the newspapers as "taking up ex-service member's jobs," no matter their own family's poverty.[23]

Biddy had her hands full overseeing Oswald's work and their daughter's girlhood, but she needed to cut her living expenses as much as possible. By 1922, the Ofvenbergs required more room. In addition, Miss Ashe had returned from the Middle East and wanted to live with Biddy and Kathleen.

Biddy prayed, listened to advice, consulted Scripture, and waited for the circumstances to indicate her next move. As long as she tarried, waiting for God's direction, she knew the right place would come. And one day, a surprising offer from someone linked to publishing turned up. All it required was a move out of London.

# 14

## Isn't There Some Misunderstanding?

### *1921–29*

Faith is deliberate commitment to a Person where I see no way.[1]

With nearly three million British casualties (900,000 dead) following World War I, two million British widows and single women were declared "surplus women" by the *London Times* and destined never to marry. A handsome woman with a witty sense of humor, extraordinary skills, and a deep spirituality, Biddy Chambers might have attracted the interest of some men over the course of her life. Living daily in her late husband's words, however, she never considered remarriage.

Every day she picked up her shorthand notes and transcribed them on her Royal typewriter. As she read, Biddy remembered the setting when she took the notes and could hear Oswald's voice, his inflections, and his laugh. In her mind, she saw his expressive face and beautiful hands once more. She could recall the heather scent, the babbling streams, the perspiration dripping down her back, the whine of mosquitoes.

Paging through letters and diaries, she often came across a line reminding her of his love: "I miss you more than breath but I am thankful you are where you are. Be unperturbed by anything. Be just yourself."[2]

What man could hope to compete with such a memory?

Oswald was not alive, yet his words were. His job was done, yet hers continued. Their daughter grew, their friends went their separate ways, but Oswald's humorous take on BTC remained a watchword for Biddy: "BTC, the Best is yet To Come."

In those dismal days of England's search for a new normal, Biddy relied on eyes of faith to believe better times were coming. Shortages continued, jobs remained scarce, and the government roiled as it struggled to cope with societal changes. With limited funds available and a need to move, Biddy's ears pricked up when a friend suggested Oxford—the home of several printing and publishing companies in the early 1920s.

Biddy, Kathleen, and Mary Riley—joining them to help with the unpacking—soon caught the steam train to travel ninety miles northwest with the Chamberses' few possessions and important trunks in the baggage car. They left the drab, tired city for a flourishing countryside green with vegetation and farming communities.

The medieval spires of Oxford's famed colleges rose above an otherwise provincial town, still cobbled in places and featuring Tudor-style buildings on the square. Scholars bicycled past with their black robes flying, while English dons C. S. Lewis and J. R. R. Tolkien met with the other Inklings for a pint at the Eagle and Child pub.

They disembarked a few miles north of Oxford in the tiny community of Yarnton. Bookseller Charles John Parker had offered Biddy a rustic cottage on his Ivy Lodge estate, perhaps in exchange for assistance with his ailing wife. He charged her a meager five shillings a week (about US $15, 2014) for the lattice-windowed bungalow—which did not have electricity or indoor plumbing. She could barely afford it. "We really didn't have anything," Kathleen said.[3]

Facing Woodstock Road, the estate featured wide fields, banks of spring periwinkles, and an overflowing vegetable garden. The Parker manservant visited the cottage every morning with freshly laid eggs and harvested vegetables. Biddy drew water in a bucket from the well for her household and relished the clean country air.[4] Once Miss Riley saw the simple household organized, she traveled back to London's St. John's Wood neighborhood and Miss Ashe, recently returned from Egypt, moved in.

Parker and his wife, Agnes, lived in the fourteen-room manor house. A once-famed beauty presented at Court to Queen Victoria, Mrs. Parker adored Saint Bernard dogs. At one point, the couple owned twenty-five canines and, from her wheelchair each morning, Mrs. Parker supervised her housekeeper walking the large friendly dogs.

She suffered from acute arthritis and often self-medicated with alcohol. Her past social opportunities had evaporated and pain gnawed at her, particularly at night.

Within days of their arrival, a late-night knock sounded on the cottage's wooden door. Biddy opened it to a lantern and an apologetic manservant. "Sorry, ma'am, the missus be needing you this night."

Biddy dashed water on her face from the bucket, checked on the sleeping Kathleen, and nodded to the vigilant Miss Ashe—who would pray. While Miss Ashe's smothering affection could be difficult to live with, her presence enabled Biddy to respond whenever Mrs. Parker needed her. (Kathleen, for her part, loved hearing Miss Ashe's incredible stories about her youth in Australia.)

Up at the big house, the invalid's frantic wails echoed as soon as Biddy entered: "Bring Mrs. Chambers up here. She's the only one who can help the pain."

Biddy spoke briefly to an anxious Charles Parker as well as Agnes's sister, Alice, before entering the sumptuous bedroom. The raving woman screamed in her misery, but her eyes lightened at Biddy's calm face. Biddy sat in the chair beside the plush bed, perhaps taking Mrs. Parker's hand. After years of comforting people, Biddy knew how to pray and read the Scriptures to soothe the woman's racing heart and soul.

Certainly Biddy remembered Oswald's comments from the BTC devotional time about God "bringing you into places and among people and into conditions in order that the intercession of the Spirit in you may take a particular line."[5]

She often sat deep into the night until Mrs. Parker quieted to sleep and Biddy could go home.

Even as Biddy helped care for his wife, Parker assisted with her daughter. He drove Kathleen to school each morning in a pony and trap. A longtime member of the British publishing world, Parker owned Parker's Bookshop on Oxford's Broad Street. "He gave me all these wonderful children's books," Kathleen said. "He was very sweet to me, a lovely old gentleman."[6]

Yarnton provided greater freedom for Kathleen than London. She romped with the dogs and ate blackberries and other wild fruit to her heart's content. The cottage dwellers walked across open fields to attend church or catch the train.

Biddy and Miss Ashe soon became weekly fixtures on the local Methodist preacher's plan. Miss Ashe rode the train to Sunday speaking engagements while Biddy bicycled into the countryside with Kathleen to preach to rural farm families. The farm wives often asked Biddy to lead the small gatherings in multiverse hymns before lunch to give them time to cook the luncheon vegetables!

With Kathleen happy and Miss Ashe on hand to help, Biddy returned to her notes. Perhaps because she sensed Chamberlain, the publisher who had decided not to work with her, hadn't truly understood the scope of Oswald's work, Biddy retyped one of his signature materials, *The Psychology of Redemption*, for release in the British market. As an extension of Oswald's *Biblical Psychology*, the book drew parallels between Christ's life and the Christian's life of faith. Published in 1922 by "The B. T. C. Publishing Committee," the book was printed and produced by Bell & Bain Ltd, a Glasgow printer/publishing house.

The B. T. C. Publishing Committee was a loose confederation of friends who had known, studied under, or appreciated Oswald. Charles and Norah Griffin headed the list, which included League of Prayer members David Lambert, Percy Lockhart, and John Skidmore. Former soldier Louis Clarke also assisted Biddy, along with Dais and Gertrude.

Meanwhile, Charles Parker advised Biddy on bookselling matters. She also made new friends, Henry and Ivy Alden of the local printing firm Alden's Press, whom she met through the Methodist preaching circuit. (Both Parker and Alden knew Griffin through publishing networks.)

In October 1924, Biddy turned to Alden Press for publication of her next project, *Shade of His Hand*. Taken from the last series of lectures Oswald gave at Zeitoun before his death, the book used Ecclesiastes to focus on the simple question, "Is life worth living apart from the Redemption?" The title came from Francis Thompson's famous poem, "The Hound of Heaven." In the foreword, Biddy included a prayer explaining her hope for all the books: "May the Spirit of God bring to all who read the book a vision of Our Lord Jesus Christ 'in whom are hid all the treasures of wisdom.'"[7]

The new publication revealed two significant changes for Biddy. While printed by Alden Press of Oxford, the book was distributed by the Commonwealth's largest book wholesaler, Simpkin Marshall of London. The introduction to Simpkin Marshall probably came through Griffin, who got his initial training in publishing at the company, though the managing director was Herbert Alden— Henry Alden's cousin.

In addition, "B. C." included a new address: 200 Woodstock Road, Oxford. After several years in the Yarnton cottage, they had moved into town for a new opportunity.

Despite her long hours at the typewriter, Biddy had few financial resources. Friends' generosity still provided for their living expenses and necessary items such as Kathleen's school fees and clothing. "We had nothing when we returned from Egypt. Everything in our home was a gift from someone," Kathleen said.[8]

While it undoubtedly made her business-minded friends cringe, not accepting pay for producing the books made spiritual sense to Biddy. She felt it was in keeping with Oswald's example of expecting God to provide for what he asked his people to do.

Biddy had worked for a living prior to marriage and may have struggled with this concept during those first years at the BTC, too, but she soon adopted Oswald's ideas concerning God and money. She and Oswald often had experienced the Lord providing needed funds in a timely manner.

When money got especially tight, Biddy called Kathleen to join her.

> "Come here with me a minute and get down on your knees. I'm going to tell the Almighty about something." . . . She would tell God that we didn't have any money. She wasn't worried, but she wanted Him to know that she trusted Him, somehow, for the money to come. And the money always came.[9]

As Kathleen neared her teenage years and became more self-conscious of appearances, however, the girl bristled at the charity. She recalled the "hot flame of anger that used to rise up in me" when well-meaning people dropped off a box, offering "clothes which might be useful to you and your mother." A furious Kathleen sometimes tossed out the torn, stained, or unfashionable garments, demanding, "How dare these people think we can wear this terrible stuff?"[10]

Biddy watched her daughter's reactions with dismay, conscious of Oswald's reminder that obedience to God might cost Kathleen more than it did Biddy herself.[11] Kathleen simply wanted to dress like her friends at school. But Biddy's conviction not to take pay for her work on the books, cemented into her belief God would provide for them materially, figuratively tied her hands. She undoubtedly remembered how, while serving as the BTC's superintendent, she specifically asked Mrs. Howard Hooker to provide *new* clothing for visiting missionaries and their families.

Oswald, of course, had always presented a well-groomed appearance and liked to see his wife and daughter dressed well. "She always loved nice things,"[12] Kathleen said, but new clothes weren't possible with Biddy's meager funds.

Kathleen's sensitivity may have motivated Biddy to make changes in her financial and living situation. While she refused to personally profit from the books, she could earn extra cash through other work done from home. Reviewing one of Oswald's encouraging letters from 1915 reminded her of an old Scots prayer: "Lord, keep me strong in the sense of Thy calling and give us our need," along with his follow-up remark: "You are the woman of God among girls heading right."[13]

So—through a friend's help—Biddy rented a roomy house on the corner of Woodstock and Beech Croft Road, a mile north of the Oxford colleges. She took in four undergraduate boarders, provided a room for Miss Ashe, and arranged a basement office for herself. As a "licensed lodging house keeper," under the auspices of the Oxford colleges, Biddy served breakfast, tea, and a three-course meal during the week and full board on weekends.[14]

Biddy rose at 6:15 each morning and said her prayers, shorthanding them into an exercise book (when she filled one book, she threw it away and started over in a new one). After her devotions, she brewed tea and distributed it to her household along with a thin slice of white bread with butter. Following their cooked breakfast, the students departed for the day and Biddy escorted Kathleen across town by bicycle to school.

Most school-aged children don't want an adult escort, but Kathleen's hand-me-down bicycle was too tall for her. Once boosted on, Kathleen would fall off the bike if she had to brake, and so Biddy pedaled with her in the mornings and met her at the schoolyard gate to ride home in the afternoons. "Very long suffering, she was," Kathleen said.[15]

Kathleen attended the Milham Ford School, located on the River Cherwell near the Oxford colleges. During her school years, Kathleen played field hockey, one of the "first eleven" players chosen for the school team. She thrived at the eight-hundred-student school and adored the wheelchair-bound headmistress.

Once a week, Kathleen attended Crusader classes in private homes. Much like a modern youth group, Crusader classes incorporated creative means to teach the Bible to students from a variety of local churches.

Kathleen grew into an angular, fair-haired girl resembling her father but struggled with her faith. "It can be a handicap to be raised in a Christian family. You imagine you know more than you do, but you only know *about* God," she explained.[16] Biddy gave her daughter room and time to find her own personal relationship with God.

Pedaling home from the morning ride to school, Biddy visited the post office, bank, grocer, butcher, and other shops, before returning to wash, bake, clean, and perform other housework. The post office stop satisfied her the most, given her extensive correspondence. With her close Zeitoun friends scattered around the world, Biddy enjoyed keeping up with what the BTC training produced in real life.

Philip and Kathleen Hancock finished seminary in California and sailed with daughter Mary to Persia, where they both served as missionaries. Eva and Stephen Pulford were at seminary in London with their daughter Mary Lois.

181

Biddy could read about the Donnithornes' 1925 adventures in the newspaper. While on holiday in western China, Gladys, Vyvyan, their two-year-old daughter Audrey, and six other missionaries were captured by Red Lantern bandits. After three weeks of forced marching, they were rescued—insect bitten and hungry, but healthy. Vyvyan wrote of the friendly country people they had encountered and hoped to return with the gospel. The Donnithornes served as missionaries in China their entire lives.

Living near the colleges meant visitors stopped by. Biddy always incorporated hospitality into her daily tasks. Whenever someone rang the bell, she set aside her plans and focused on her guest. She brewed a pot of tea, sat down, and listened. As Biddy explained to her daughter, "we must give the day over into God's hands, completely, so that He will look after who comes."[17]

"She was a person always very mindful of everybody's creature comforts," Kathleen said. "She wanted people to feel comfortable, well fed and at home."[18]

Douglas Downes called frequently. Originally of the Church of England, Downes had served as a YMCA padre at the Cairo citadel during the war. (His collie had often stayed with the Chambers family.) The former Oxford economics don repatriated to England and became a Franciscan friar. Wearing a brown robe tied with string and carrying a "Billy can" for food handouts, he was called "Brother Downes" and wandered the English countryside for weeks at a time. With a simple trust and belief in God, Downes wanted to live among and minister to the down-and-out (often former soldiers).

Whenever his wanderings brought him to Oxford, Downes first stopped at the Chambers home for a bath and a good meal before proceeding to the colleges to lecture. He gave Hebrew lessons, counseled students, and preached. His work attracted interest, and he spoke on his experiences at St. George Chapel before the king and queen.[19]

Once she dealt with the day's chores and interruptions, Biddy descended to her paper-filled office to work on the project now claiming her attention: a year-long devotional using excerpts from Oswald's teachings.

Biddy began the new book with a quote from nineteenth-century Scottish preacher Robert Murray McCheyne: "Men return again and again to the few who have mastered the spiritual secret, whose life has been hid with Christ in God." She explained why Oswald's words were important in the next paragraph: "The author [Oswald] is one to whose teaching men will return . . . and it is sent out with the prayer that day by day the messages may continue to bring the quickening life and inspiration of the Holy Spirit."[20]

Early in the process, Biddy discussed the idea with Henry Alden of Alden Press, and he told her to bring him the manuscript when she finished it. His enthusiasm sustained her as the new book required an extensive read through all her notes, hunting for Oswald's most significant remarks. It took three years to assemble.

Biddy patterned her book as a daily devotional capable of standing alongside popular versions already in print, including her favorite, the *Daily Light*.

The *Daily Light* readings had often spoken to both Biddy and Oswald. The couple referenced the biblical passages found in the daily readings in their letters and diaries, particularly to confirm decisions about God's work in their lives. The Bible verses didn't take long to read, but as the Word of God is sharper than a two-edged sword and goes to the marrow, reading even a small nugget twice a day brought solace and encouragement to the reader.

The *Daily Light* had been put together by a committee—thirteen members of the Bagster family during their devotional time over several years in the mid-1870s.

Charles Spurgeon had published three devotionals in the nineteenth century, including *Morning and Evening: Daily Readings*. He presented a short Bible verse followed by a one-paragraph commentary designed to strengthen a reader's relationship with God.

In the United States, Lettie Cowman's *Streams in the Desert* first appeared in 1925. Each day's passage began with a Bible verse, included Lettie's thoughts, and ended with a pertinent quotation from a sermon, poem, or other writing personally meaningful to her.

Biddy designed the new book for use alongside the Bible. She wrote a title, quoted a snippet from a Bible verse—usually less than ten words—and then added two or three paragraphs (often taken from several lectures) to augment and underscore the verse's theme.

Biddy used Oswald's words, but her mind compiled the passages and arranged them by day. The new book's title came from one of Oswald's "signature" remarks: "We have to realize that no effort can be too high. . . . It must be my utmost for His highest all the time."[21]

She began by praying—always the greater work. Biddy may have focused on themes Oswald often used, such as prayer, God's guidance, and intimacy with Christ. (See the appendix for further insight into how devotionals are written and for a deeper discussion of *My Utmost for His Highest*.)

Kathleen said the placement of some readings was deliberate, which makes sense.[22] A close reading of the text shows that Biddy revealed her emotions concerning her relationship to God and her husband on significant days. It's interesting to examine what she placed on her birthday, for example, and particularly what she chose for Oswald's day of death.

For her July 13th birthday, the reading referenced Isaiah 6:1 ("I saw also the LORD"). Using Oswald's words from a 1912 BTC teaching, she perhaps described for the only time her reaction to Oswald's death. The poignant passage says:

> Our soul's history with God is frequently the history of the "passing of the hero." Over and over again God has to remove our friends in order to bring Himself in their place, and that is where we faint and fail and get discouraged.

Take it personally: In the year that the one who stood to me for all that God was, died—I gave up everything? I became ill? I got disheartened? Or—I saw the Lord?

It must be God first, God second and God third, until the life is faced steadily with God and no one else is of any account whatever. . . . In all the world there is none but thee, my God, there is none but thee.

Oswald died, but did she get discouraged? She pressed on until she saw the Lord. (Though, as noted earlier, Biddy did come down with jaundice.) From that vision, she secured her life in one place: her hope in God and no one else.

For Oswald's July 24th birthday, the reading rested on the quality of Oswald's character: "Disposition and Deeds" from Matthew 5:20 of his Sermon on the Mount talks: "The characteristic of a disciple is not that he does good things, but that he is good in motive. . . . The only thing that exceeds right-doing is right-being."

Right-being before God was Oswald's aim.

Their wedding day provoked a wistful reflection, taken from the Genesis passage where Abraham allows Lot to choose which part of Canaan he wants. Oswald taught on Genesis during the spring of 1915, when he wrestled with the decision about his role in the war. Biddy participated in that prayerful struggle.

Biddy used the passage to reflect on choices:

As soon as you begin to live the life of faith in God, fascinating and luxurious prospects will open up before you, and these things are yours by right; but if you are living the life of faith you will exercise your right to waive your rights, and let God choose for you.

God sometimes allows you to get into a place of testing where your own welfare would be the right and proper thing to consider if you were not living a life of faith; but if you are, you will joyfully waive your right and leave God to choose for you.

Her marriage to Oswald opened the world to Biddy, literally in the sense she had traveled to two continents with him but also through the opportunities to see God's hand at work in people's lives in extraordinary fashion.

But then Oswald died, the marriage was interrupted, and Biddy had a choice—to accept Oswald's death and move on, believing God planned for her to be a widow, or to fight against God's redirection of her life. She accepted Oswald's death and remained faithful to God. Perhaps, too, this passage explained about the financial testing she lived with.

The November 15 passage addressed the question she probably heard more than any: Why did God allow Oswald to die?

The unflinching biblical text from John 21:21–22 went to the heart: "Lord, and what shall this man do? . . . What is that to thee? Follow thou me." The opening line said it all: "One of our severest lessons comes from the stubborn refusal to see that we must not interfere in other people's lives."

The reading asked who we think we are to question what God decides should happen in another person's life. (Similar to God's words to Job.) Biddy selected the passage from talks Oswald gave in Zeitoun during the first six months of 1916. Biddy's desire was for God's will to come to pass; she prayed and allowed him to mold her reaction until she could praise God no matter the circumstances.

She chose to believe God. She chose to break her independent way of thinking and be a bondservant of Jesus—advanced Christianity born of focusing on God's desires, not her own.

It's worth noting that the next day's title on November 16 also may contain a message: "Still Human," with a text from 1 Corinthians 10:31: "whatsoever ye do, do all to the glory of God." Biddy used it, perhaps, to indicate she, too, missed her husband even in the midst of clinging to God. "It is one thing to go through a crisis grandly, but another thing to go through every day glorifying God when there is no witness, no limelight, no one paying the remotest attention to us."

She labored in obscurity—on purpose. Her name never appeared in any of the Oswald Chambers books beyond her initials, B. C.

Unlike the Bagster family, Biddy had no editor or proofreader to help her with the devotional. All responsibility for the book lay in Biddy's mind, heart, and fingers—and with the Holy Spirit.

Certainly the members of the unofficial BTC Publishing committee offered advice and prayers, as well as her family. Teenaged Kathleen, however, paid little attention.

> She never talked about the books to me. She didn't want me to have anything to do with the books. I was going to be a nurse and the books were her job. . . . But my mother got the books out into print and she typed and retyped and typed and typed and she read all the proofs herself.[23]

In 1927, Biddy asked for donations to pay for the book's publication. Dorothy Docking, then twenty-six, remembered sending her pocket money, as did countless others. By the time she finished preparing the manuscript to her satisfaction, Biddy had sufficient funds in hand to pay Alden Press to publish the first edition.

Once Alden Press produced the devotion book (printing and binding), they returned it to Biddy for distribution. She passed that task on to Simpkin and Marshall. As Simpkin and Marshall dealt with trade books, *My Utmost for His Highest*, and ultimately all of Oswald's books, appeared in London bookstores, on kiosks, and in print ads. First published in England in October 1927, *My Utmost for His Highest* was popular from the start.

It has never been out of print.

# 15

## The Worker's Ruling Passion

### *1929–39*

Being ambitious only to be pleasing to Him.[1]

*B*iddy launched *My Utmost for His Highest* into a rapidly evolving world. The first transatlantic telephone call to North America took place in 1927, along with the founding of the British Television Society. Automatic traffic lights appeared on street corners and, after seventy years, lexicographers finally published *The Oxford English Dictionary*. Biddy oversaw her lodgers through the 1927–28 school term and possibly the next. The year 1929, however, brought major changes to the women living at 200 Woodstock Road.

The sixty-four-year-old Miss Ashe remained concerned for the poor in Egypt. Perhaps through letters from George Swan, soldiering on with the EGM, she learned of an organization working to improve conditions there. Determined to help women and children trapped in Cairo's red-light district, she applied for a position with the International Bureau for the Suppression of the Traffic in Women and Children (IBS). "It was incredibly dangerous what she did," Kathleen said later. She required police protection because so many of the brothels were owned by powerful men.[2]

Miss Ashe sailed for Egypt in July 1929. She listed Biddy's new address on the embarkation papers as her English home: 40 Church Crescent N 10, Muswell Hill.

Biddy had closed the boarding house and left Oxford.

While she worked on *My Utmost for His Highest*, Biddy periodically traveled to London to stay with her ailing mother. Aging Emily's illnesses required more attention and Dais needed her sister's help. Dais and Emily had rented a house eight miles directly north of Big Ben in Muswell Hill, and that is where Biddy joined them in 1929.

Located on a hillside overlooking London proper all the way to the River Thames, Muswell Hill possessed a railroad line into the city. The downtown featured churches, shops, and even an art deco–style cinema. The tree-lined streets fanned out into neighborhoods of Edwardian townhouses.

A three-story brick house with a fine garden, 40 Church Crescent was a quarter of a mile from St. James Church and two doors down from the Quaker meetinghouse. With bedrooms for the women upstairs, Biddy arranged an office where she could type and still be available for Emily. Two nights a week Biddy hosted a Bible study in the bay-windowed front parlor.

By this point, Oswald had been dead for more than a decade, yet Biddy lived with his voice ringing in her memory every single day. Her ease in mentioning him, particularly to Kathleen, made him seem far closer than the Old Cairo grave. "They loved each other very much indeed and their relationship was a wonderful relationship," Kathleen said. "She would always talk about my father as if he'd only just gone upstairs or something."[3] Owing to her mother's health, Biddy enrolled fifteen-year-old Kathleen in boarding school.[4] Kathleen did not stay long at school, finishing her education at sixteen. She then obtained a position in the Bermondsey Medical Mission Hospital, not far from the docks.[5]

Originally founded in 1904, the medical clinic and eight-bed hospital provided spiritual and medical assistance to women and children who lived in the poverty-choked East End. Kathleen helped the nursing staff deal with both minor ailments and bad accidents from the local tanneries and pickle factories. In addition to emergency medical services and care such as midwifery, the mission gave away food.

Kathleen loved children, and from childhood wanted to be a nurse. After two years at the mission hospital, where she gained an understanding of what a medical career entailed, she enrolled in the King's Hospital nursing program. There she acquired both classroom and clinical nursing experience, took anatomy and patient care classes, and helped on the wards.

Work at the mission and hospital caused Kathleen to reevaluate her faith. "I realized I only knew *about* God." At King's she saw women in misery like she'd never imagined. "You have to square everything up," Kathleen said. "I had to read the Bible . . . and come to know God in my way . . . you have to understand that He's there whatever He allows to happen."[6]

Personally engaged with her faith for the first time, Kathleen taught a Bible study to the neighborhood children and counseled her fellow nurses. She traveled home to visit her mother, aunt, and grandmother on a regular basis. The Church Crescent house, with its piano and comfortable Victorian furnishings, felt like a different and far more comfortable world than the East End. A maturing Kathleen and her grandmother could enjoy each other's company now.

Biddy pounded on her typewriter every day. In 1929 she invested the earnings from *My Utmost for His Highest* into a booklet called *Our Brilliant Heritage*. As a series on "The Gospel Mystery of Sanctification," the articles first appeared in the mid-1920s in the League of Prayer magazine *Spiritual Life*. Biddy also arranged for the publication of a fourth edition of Oswald's *Studies in the Sermon on the Mount*.

Confident in her system, Biddy discerned what to publish by prayer, salability—to keep the cash flowing—and evaluation of what people wanted to read. She arranged for reprinting *The Psychology of Redemption*, which showed parallels between the life of Christ and the Christian's life of faith, in 1930.

That year also saw publication of *So Send I You: A Series of Missionary Studies*. With a foreword written by Cairo missionary Samuel Zwemer, the book examined how a missionary could recognize their call, how to prepare for the mission, and what missionary life entailed. Zwemer thought the readings spoke to the surrendered life needed to be a missionary. The chapters mostly came from talks Oswald gave at the BTC.

Biddy also put together a series of short books about Christian habits and experience, *As He Walked* (1930) and *Grow Up into Him* (1931), and used messages on suffering and difficulties for *The Message of Invincible Consolations* (1931).

These messages may have been pertinent to her life. While Biddy's daughter grew into a young adult with adventures of her own, Biddy's mother was dying.

With all three of her children at her side, Emily Amelia Gardner Hobbs died on August 31, 1934, of complications from pneumonia and heart issues. The master baker's daughter and clerk's widow, who had lived through so many changes, was eighty-four years old. Biddy dedicated that year's book, *Not Knowing Whither*, to her mother, "whose interest in sending forth of my husband's message has been an unfailing source of inspiration."[7] She would miss her.

By 1932, the scope of Biddy's publishing work encompassed not only editorial responsibilities and letter writing but also other projects designed for missionaries in the field. An African Inland Mission missionary's remark lodged in Biddy's heart: "Out on the field we are like a lot of hens scratching for ourselves."[8] Oswald had dreamed of visiting mission stations, or places where missionaries vacationed, to refresh and teach them—refilling the spiritual wells, as it were, of those who spent their lives sharing the gospel.

One of the BTC committee advisors, Reverend David Lambert, had known and admired Oswald. A keen teacher, he volunteered to assist Biddy with a monthly journal using material from the BTC lectures and the correspondence course. Designed as a type of refresher course, continuing education, and encouragement for missionaries in the field, the *Bible Training Course Monthly Journal* was born.

Volume one, number one, appeared in April 1932. In the foreword, written to all former students of the Bible Training College, Biddy and Lambert sent a message of "good cheer, and a hearty reminder BTC still stands as our watchword, viz: 'Better to Come.'"[9] Oswald's old red signature stamp followed the words at the bottom of the front page.

Volume two, number one began with text taken from BTC sermon class lectures. Seven pages followed, with a note from Lambert setting the discussion question, "How can I keep Christ's commands?" along with his address and a request to include a self-addressed stamped envelope if they wanted their paper returned with comments. They used Oswald's *Sermon on the Mount* as a textbook. The worldwide circulation soon reached seven hundred.

Biddy's responsibilities, of course, focused on the content gleaned from her notes.

By this time, Biddy clearly ran a small publishing house; in today's publishing lingo it would best be described as "boutique" since it focused solely on Oswald's writings. Businesses require a ready source of capital to keep them afloat and publishing is no exception. (Twenty years later, British editor Diana Athill would help found the Allan Wingate publishing house and, observing conventional wisdom of the time, insisted a publishing house could not be started on less than £3000 and required £15,000 a year to run the operation.)[10] As she always used the funds received from the books to produce more books, Biddy watched her cash flow carefully.

It's worth noting Biddy did not advertise the books beyond one simple announcement in Christian periodicals and a list of all the published works in the back of the books or the *BTC Monthly Journal*.

Sixty-year-old Gertrude Chambers now lived alone in the Dulwich flat. (Hannah died in 1921 and Clarence in 1925.) Gertrude added the distribution and mailings of the *BTC Monthly Journal* to her tasks. When asked, Gertrude referred to herself as a secretary to a publishing house—which exactly described her role.

Biddy frequently received letters asking for information about Oswald—and since his name appeared on the cover and title pages of his books, some correspondents assumed they wrote directly to him. Many asked for biographical information. In pondering her project for 1933, Biddy believed a biography would "lead to a fuller apprehension of the truths he taught," and demonstrate how he had lived out those truths.[11]

She spent months on a project she titled *Oswald Chambers: His Life and Work*. The "two-fold thread" she emphasized as running through the book came from two specific quotes from Oswald: "If I have an ambition, it is that I might have honorable mention in anyone's personal relationship with Our Lord Jesus Christ," and "One life may be of incalculable use to God: and yours may be that life."[12]

Once again, Biddy sorted through stacks of papers, particularly his diaries, as she edited and collated a variety of material. She appealed to friends for their stories about Oswald as well, which was a different approach for this book.

For information about her husband's youth, Biddy appealed to his brother. Franklin, a few years older than Gertrude (who didn't write anything), provided many stories for the first section.

When his remembrances ended, Biddy filled out the early years with memories from friends, excerpts from letters, and lengthy passages from Oswald's diary.

Biddy followed the same pattern through all six sections of the biography, carefully keeping the focus on Oswald or his words. She ended with her own memories of the final weeks of her husband's life and how the book ministry grew out of their time in Zeitoun. Charles Rae Griffin concluded the first edition with a short description of how the Oswald Chambers books came to be, followed by a list of availability and price.

Ultimately, the biography sold about fifteen thousand copies in three editions, but a disappointed Biddy felt the sales did not reflect the amount of work required to produce it. The book also stirred troubling emotions. "It meant a tremendous lot of hard work," Kathleen explained, "but [writing] the book only revealed to her how little she knew about my father, really. All his early life was lost where she was concerned."[13] (It is also worth noting Biddy's sense of loss may have been aggravated by the recent death of her mother.)

Biddy saw the amount of interest and the sale of the books as an indicator of what should be produced. "If you spend money on something that isn't going to sell, it's typing money up," Kathleen said. "You had to have a certain number [sell] to make it worthwhile."[14]

In 1932, the BTC Committee advisors decided to charter themselves into an official group called the Oswald Chambers Publication Association (OCPA). The original members were Percy Lockhart (a prosperous Dunstable coal merchant from the League of Prayer days and Oswald's best man), Charles Griffin (inevitable; still living in London and director of Griffin and Sons Publishing), Louis R. S. Clarke (a Zeitoun soldier turned accountant living in Devon), Gertrude, and Dais.

Biddy recognized her need for assistance but had a few stipulations. As Stephen Pulford later wrote in an article in *The Life of Faith* magazine:

> The members considered it their responsibility to handle the business side of affairs and to some extent watch over Mrs. Chambers' interests; but she, as chairman, made it a condition she must continue as in the past to be free to give books to whomsoever she felt led. Many thousands of books were thus given or sent by post free of cost, many to people she didn't know, but whom she felt might be helped by them.[15]

Members of the committee loved Biddy and Kathleen; most had supported them since the BTC days. As they met monthly to discuss items related to the books, they helped make decisions. An example of the scope of their involvement can be seen in the June 1934 minutes, where they discussed the style of type Alden's would use, how big the order of books should be, and the cost of producing five thousand books. Was £187.5 a good price if it included paper, printing, binding, and a book jacket?[16]

Pointing out the house and taxes were a business expense, since Biddy's home functioned as both the headquarters and storehouse of Oswald Chambers publications, the OCPA committee eventually assumed those expenses—especially when the balance sheet showed sufficient funds in hand. They tried to pay Biddy a salary, but she refused.

When they insisted, Biddy accepted only a minimum sum to cover her rental costs and used the house as an open source for ministry. The committee then voted her a modest yearly entertainment allowance, trying to provide her some income. She turned the tables on them by insisting upon cooking a hot lunch or dinner as part of the monthly OCPA meetings.

Lengthy discussions concerning translation rights, binding qualities, interest in translating the books—usually *My Utmost for His Highest*—filled the minutes. The members weighed the value of one type of binding over another and which company provided the best price. They debated paper quality and whether or not they should produce a cheaper version of *My Utmost for His Highest*. Year by year, the ministry's success could be seen in the growing number of translations of *My Utmost for His Highest*: Afrikaans, German, French, Finnish, Chinese, and Estonian.

The committee occasionally produced an especially fine edition of *My Utmost for His Highest* for presentation purposes. In 1936, Brother Douglas Downes delivered a special edition to his "friends" King George V and Queen Mary. The OCPA received a May 8 thank-you letter from the Queen's secretary:

> I am commanded by Queen Mary to thank you most gratefully for the very charming little book which you have so kindly sent to Her Majesty.
>
> Various people at different times have sent the Queen books of daily readings, but this one seems quite different from the ordinary more stereotyped variety, and I think Her Majesty will read it with real interest and I hope comfort.
>
> The Queen is much touched by your kind thought and also by the trouble you have taken in having it so beautifully bound. Her Majesty sends you all good wishes for your splendid work.[17]

Jimmy Hanson joined the OCPA committee in 1936 and the minutes mention ways other former BTC students helped from around the world. BTC alumni Isabel Craddock, a missionary in India, reviewed the Hindi translation, for example. When Biddy asked former students serving as missionaries to describe their experiences for the *BTC Monthly Journal*, alumni wrote from the Belgian Congo, India, China, South Africa, Canada, France, Australia, Persia, West Ivory Coast, Ireland, the United States, London, and a variety of British towns. Certainly, their memories encouraged Biddy and make interesting reading today.

The minutes frequently revealed how Biddy's heart centered on missionaries, and she periodically requested the OCPA make gifts to specific missions—usually in £10 increments.

No one knows how many copies of *My Utmost for His Highest* sold, but Biddy got so much mail about the books the Muswell Hill post office finally gave "Mrs. Oswald Chambers" her own slot for sorting purposes. She regularly received and responded to up to fifty letters a day. Biddy often typed her responses because her handwriting so often drifted into a modified shorthand that was impossible for the average person to read. After forty years of typing on her Royal typewriter, Biddy needed to buy a new one in the 1930s.

When their Church Crescent lease ended in 1937, Biddy and Dais moved half a mile north to Woodberry Crescent. It was another three-story brick home with a lovely garden in back, and Biddy quickly established herself in the neighborhood. She regularly took treats to new neighbors, opened her house for Bible study, and befriended a group of children who would stop by for tea or to play in her garden. Kathleen soon discovered the children also came for breakfast, with the obliging Biddy minding the stove and pouring the milk. "They thought she was the cat's whiskers," Kathleen said.[18]

Kathleen moved home during this time. While working at King's Hospital she had contracted tuberculosis, as did many nurses during that era. In her case, the tuberculosis settled in her gut, not her lungs, leaving her thin and very sick, thus ending her nurse's training. A friend took her to a sanitarium in Switzerland and another escorted her to Germany. It took Kathleen nearly five years to recover, but once well, she returned home.

One day, a nurse friend from Bermondsey visited and suggested that—for her own sake and those of needy people—Kathleen return to the mission. Kathleen agreed, and later observed, "I worked there harder than I've ever worked in my life."[19] She taught a Bible class to teenagers and young children living in the East End, and often brought them home for a cup of tea and cakes with her mother. Kathleen's students adored Biddy—who enjoyed their rambunctious visits.

The 1930s were good years. When not typing in her office, Biddy often could be found brewing tea and chatting with a neighbor, a visitor, or the local children (who called her "Mrs. Biddy").

The neighbors got used to seeing unusual strangers knocking on Biddy's door. "It was really quite something to see a great big African in his own kind of clothes and his wife walking down the Crescent. They wore turbans on their head," Kathleen said. "Everyone knew they would only be coming here. It caused quite a sensation. Nobody had friends who were Sioux Indians and Africans."[20]

Biddy's sense of humor always bubbled beneath her calm exterior. Theology students frequently visited for food and fellowship. When a group of solemn students came to dinner one night, the conversation sagged under the heaviness of their topics. Despite having several of Kathleen's vivacious girlfriends in for the same meal, the evening dragged.

Biddy finally picked up a cherry from the bowl in the center of the table. "Kathleen, why don't you and Margaret and Sheila see if you can spit cherry stones on to the top of the mantelpiece on that side of the table?" she said.[21]

With little urging, the young men joined the fun and salvaged the evening.

Mrs. Howard Taylor (daughter-in-law of China Inland missionary Hudson Taylor) was another frequent visitor. "She was always so amazed my mother never stopped doing anything,"[22] Kathleen said. Mary Guinness Taylor shut herself away in the country for fourteen years to write her biography of Hudson Taylor, and yet while Biddy compiled her books she never stopped doing all the ordinary things like shopping, cooking, and washing.

Guests appreciated Biddy's warmth, and more than once missionaries asked her to board their children while they served in foreign countries. Remembering Oswald's admonition to care for their daughter herself, Biddy always said no.

People regularly traveled to Muswell Hill seeking her advice. Kathleen described coming home one day to a Rolls-Royce parked in front, the chauffeur waiting.

Biddy was pouring hot water into a teapot when Kathleen found her in the kitchen. An elegant woman sat at the table overlooking the garden, staring into her empty cup. She met Kathleen's eye. "I've had a wonderful time here with your mother." The woman sighed. "I used to read *My Utmost for His Highest* all the time. I'm in great trouble and I needed to talk with your mother in this situation out here in the kitchen." She picked up her fork and touched a crumb of the homemade cake on a plate before her.

Biddy indicated Kathleen should disappear.

"Who was that?" Kathleen asked after the woman departed in the expensive auto.

Biddy never betrayed a confidence. The wife of a prominent member of the royal household had a personal problem and sought counsel. Biddy had listened, turned her hands up to God, and given the problem to him. Her simple prayer and confidence in God cheered the mysterious woman and gave her hope for another day.

"A lot of people did that," Kathleen said.[23]

Biddy's ministry of interruptions continued, as valuable as ever.

Especially with war once again on the horizon.

# 16

## The Teaching of Adversity

### 1939–46

God never gives strength for tomorrow, or for the next hour,
but only for the strain of the minute.[1]

*W*hile her hair turned white and her body slowed, Biddy
Chambers remained active in her life and her publishing house. She typed as fast as ever, wrote out her many prayers
in shorthand, and contemplated the *Daily Light* every morning.

She and Dais lived easily with each other. They enjoyed concerts
at Queen's Hall and Albert Hall, as well as attended a nearby
church every Wednesday night, and occasionally visited St. Martin
in the Fields to hear Oswald's brother Franklin play the organ.

Biddy read the newspaper from front to back each day, especially enjoying Winston Churchill's writing as her keen mind followed world and political events. On nights she and Dais weren't
holding a Bible study, they read—Agatha Christie's mysteries and
John Buchan's suspense novels were among their favorites. First

published in 1915, Buchan's story of spies in Scotland, *The 39 Steps*, was amusing, but by 1939 perhaps felt a bit too plausible.

England still reeled from the worldwide depression and Germany's sabers rattled in alarming ways—the German leader's shrill voice assaulted wireless listeners' ears and unnerved them. While working to maintain peace, the British government began to prepare their nation for a possible war.

Blackout restrictions went into effect on September 1, 1939. Wardens wearing tin helmets and carrying whistles patrolled neighborhoods nightly to ensure no light leaked from buildings. BBC television towers were an easy target, so the fledgling television channels went off the air for the duration of the hostilities. BBC radio no longer reported the weather forecast because the information could be valuable to the enemy. Cloaked automobile headlamps and darkened streetlights made roadways dangerous. People stayed home at night and read. Church attendance increased.

When German troops moved into the Rhineland, Austria, and Czechoslovakia, citizens agonized about another war. *Kristallnacht*'s book burning only increased fears. The OCPA minutes of 1939 referenced concerns for refugees across the continent and recounted how friends had bought up German editions of *My Utmost for His Highest* and stashed them in Switzerland.

Many were uneasy and frightened, which may be why Biddy published *The Graciousness of Uncertainty*—a book dealing with faith and facing the unknown. Miss Ashe, no stranger to uncertainty and danger, wrote the foreword from Cairo, pointing readers toward the need for spiritual grace.

Invariably, Biddy's thoughts returned to the BTC days, when Oswald weighed his role in war. He'd preached on the "Psalms of Ascent" (Psalms 120–34), during their final summer at Askrigg in 1915. In reviewing those notes, Biddy saw in them encouragement for such a time and place as England during the "phony war" of fall and winter 1939. Biddy compiled Oswald's observations into

*The Pilgrim's Song Book*, released in 1940. Once again, Miss Ashe wrote a foreword from Cairo, this time observing, "only the stern business of holding the eternal values in the strange world . . . is left us as our task."[2]

Oswald's opening comments on Psalm 121 explain the importance of the book: "The Bible deals with terrors and upsets, with people who have got into despair . . . and yet all through is the uncrushable certainty that in the end everything will be all right."[3]

Biddy experienced a major change in early 1940 when Dais surprised her with an announcement: "I'll be moving soon."

Biddy stopped typing. "Where are you going?"

Her sixty-one-year-old sister blushed. "Dunstable. Percy asked me to marry him."

A widower since 1934, Percy Lockhart had known Dais since Oswald and Biddy's 1910 wedding. He had served as best man and Dais had stood up for her sister on that long-ago May day. They worked together as members of the OCPA. Percy's only child had enlisted in the military. The coal merchant's big house, Cordova, rattled empty; the calm and loving Dais could fill it well.

A hug and a kiss from Biddy indicated her approval, and they arranged a simple wedding. Percy and Dais married in March—the same month the German *Luftwaffe* first bombed the British Royal Navy base at Scotland's Scapa Flow.

The British publishing industry scrambled to deal with the potential effects of war early in 1940. Designed by industry professionals, War Risks Insurance sought to mitigate individual publishers' financial catastrophe in case of an enemy attack. Unfortunately, the insurance was expensive. Required for ownership of goods valued at more than £1000 (about US $60,000, 2014),[4] the policy assessed rates based on the total monetary value of the stock in hand. As industry publication *The Bookseller* noted, "The terms of this scheme are of deep concern to the book trade, which carries an unusually heavy stock in relation to its turnover. Publishers in particular will be gravely affected."[5]

In other words, publishers had to pay insurance based not on what it cost them to produce physical books but on the much higher valuation of their potential sale price. *The Bookseller* observed that, as a result, booksellers would have to increase the price of books in order to pay the insurance on unsold books.

All publishers, including the OCPA, faced a crisis in another crucial area: paper shortages. With the fall of France, paper manufacturers lost access to the commodities essential to making paper. The British government mandated a license to buy paper and attached quotas to the amounts available to publishing houses. They fixed the rationing rate at 60 percent of the total paper a publishing house purchased between September 1938 and August 1939. (Restrictions, however, did not apply to the government itself. They used mountains of paper to print regulations, ration cards, warnings, military training manuals, and the like.)

The OCPA's value to Biddy became apparent at their July 1940 meeting. Businessman/brother-in-law Percy reported on information obtained through the Liverpool London and Globe Insurance Company as to whether the unsold Oswald Chambers books came under the obligatory section of the War Risks Insurance Act.

He read aloud letters from Simpkin Marshall Publishing discussing fire insurance on the stock they held, while Butler and Tanner Printing explained the books and molds (a type of printing plate) in their possession were *not* insured. This basically meant none of the Oswald Chambers books were insured under the provisions of the new government insurance act.

After a lengthy discussion, the committee decided if the Chambers publications fell under the "required to insure" section of the act, of course they would do so. Otherwise, in "accordance with the teaching of the books" (to trust that God designed all events, including potential catastrophes, according to his plan), they would not insure the books. The committee directed Percy to write Simpkin Marshall stating if a fire occurred there, the OCPA would not make a claim for the stock in the warehouses, even if circumstances caused them to regret the decision.[6]

Butler and Tanner Printing also informed the committee the British government had requisitioned a large block of their warehouse. As a result, the OCPA needed to find alternate storage for the Oswald Chambers books held by the printing company.

Faced with the inability to obtain all the paper they wanted and recognizing the need to make changes, the OCPA altered the *BTC Monthly Journal* publication schedule to bimonthly until the end of the hostilities. They also examined their inventory to ensure sufficient availability of the most popular books.

Despite these mounting business tensions, Biddy maintained her active personal life and ministry. She met with her Bible study and Oswald book groups and used a prayer journal called *Thine Is the Kingdom: A Book of Prayers for Use in Time of War* by Canon Normal H. Clarke of Southwark Cathedral. It's interesting to read the prayer lists, starting with the king and queen. On the second page she wrote the names of soldiers, many of them sons of close friends or loved ones in their own right, like her nephew Jack Hobbs, Jimmy Hanson's two sons, and the Swan boys from Zeitoun. Page three's list included missionaries serving in dangerous places and the Salvation Army. Even US General George Patton and President Harry Truman made the roster.[7]

Biddy prayed first thing every morning not only for friends around the world but for her daughter working in harm's way.

The *Luftwaffe* bombed London proper for the first time on September 7, 1940, and flew bombing runs for most of the next year. Targeting initially focused on the dockyard and Parliament buildings but soon spread to other areas. In the East End, Kathleen worked at Islington Medical Mission near the Thames River. Bombed out more than once, the medical teams set up wherever they could find space, including behind a bakery at one point, before settling beneath the Islington Congregational Church.

In her late twenties, Kathleen worked hard. "We were very badly bombed in Islington," she said. "We had a mission house there and a very large time bomb fell outside the mission and we had to be evacuated." Bombs continually fell and chaos ruled the area. Evacuated several times because of both time bombs and land mines, Kathleen and her colleagues salvaged what they could with their own hands—even with bombs still ticking nearby. "Everyone pulled together and it was really very exciting," she said.[8]

Many of Kathleen's friends were nurses, and as different hospitals (where they lived in quarters) were bombed, her friends sought refuge at Biddy's house. "My mother had to look after about eight or nine of us, I suppose, all together every night." As the Woodberry Crescent house lacked a basement, the women simply piled another mattress on the parlor floor whenever someone new sought refuge.

"It was always difficult to leave my mother, especially at night time," Kathleen said. "As a rule there were lots of people here [at the house], but we never knew if I'd come home again, because it was very difficult down there [in Islington]." Too often she went to visit a friend only to turn the corner and discover the entire block had been bombed flat. Londoners of that time were stoic and uncomplaining, she noted. "My mother had a saying when we'd had a muddle somewhere, 'Praise the Lord, we're all nice and safe again.'"[9]

Several bombs plummeted into Muswell Hill that fall, only a block from Biddy's home. She described the experience in a letter to Eva Spink Pulford: "Last night about 1:30 a most awful crash and roar and everything shook and the window was flung open and then swung back and no glass broken—both sides of us have most of them smashed."[10]

The bomb fell behind the block on Queen's Avenue, where many of the large homes were destroyed. Those remaining lost all the window glass and sustained severe damage. Nearby Princess Avenue lost two shops. Biddy wrote, "Seeing it all is as bad as hearing it, but it is made possible to look at the things not seen, so the seen things don't dominate."

Despite the upsetting night, she held her afternoon class on the philosophy of discernment. Unsurprisingly, only three people attended. Meanwhile, Kathleen went to the mission, "at least to the place where it was, for it was swept out of existence by a land mine last night. . . . They will carry on somewhere near and K. phoned there is lots to do."

Biddy had never fretted about Zeppelins over London in the previous war; indeed, her war experiences in Egypt were completely different from that of her family in England. In 1939 she faced the possibility of bombings with aplomb: "I am glad we are constrained to stay on and prove His keeping, it was a truly wonderful experience. Psalm 84 for tonight, we shall 'pass through this valley, and meantime find Him a shield.'"

Apparently given an opportunity to evacuate, "the guidance seems to be just to keep around and do the obvious things and each day brings its own confirmation of this." She expressed relief, however, about a storm coming—the brilliant moons of recent evenings had made the bombings possible.

Frightening though exploding bombs in her backyard may have been, the most significant German run under a bomber's moon occurred on the 114th night of the Blitz: December 29, 1940.

London booksellers had gathered on and around the western steps of St. Paul's Cathedral to hawk their wares since the sixteenth century. Four hundred years later, British publishers located their offices on nearby Paternoster Row, along with their book warehouses. The signature London Blitz photo shows St. Paul's Cathedral rising from the smoke that December night. Fire wardens constantly on guard protected the cathedral by putting out any fires, but twenty-four thousand high explosives and one hundred thousand incendiary bombs fell around it. The famous photo depicted not the burning of the cathedral but of British publishing warehouses—or in *The Bookseller's* words, "the crematories of the city's book world."[11]

One million books went up in smoke. Water from firehoses turned any paper surviving the inferno into soggy pulp. Simpkin Marshall burned to the ground that night, taking with it forty thousand warehoused Oswald Chambers books. Simpkin Marshall's records, though stored in a safe, sat underwater for several days and were ruined.

The grim January 25, 1941, meeting of the OCPA centered on the future of the publications work. Described as a "very full discussion," the meeting lasted a long time as they sorted out what had happened, what they knew, and what they suspected. Accountant Louis Clarke, who handled the finances, had written Simpkin Marshall's general manager for information but the undoubtedly besieged man had not yet replied.

Percy Lockhart owned Simpkin Marshall Company stock. That very morning he had received a letter announcing that reconstruction of the company would not take place. Thanks to a trade organization agreement worked out between the British government and other publishing houses, Book Centre Ltd. had assumed the name, goodwill, organization, and wholesale distribution of Simpkin Marshall's stock. For the most part, Simpkin Marshall would spend the rest of its existence sorting through and settling claims from the December 29 firebombing.

Percy once more asked if the committee didn't think they should insure what stock they still had. Clarke pointed out the books remaining at Butler and Tanner (they hadn't moved them yet) were valued at approximately £800. The committee, therefore, had no obligation to purchase War Risks Insurance as required by the government's £1000 threshold.

Biddy maintained a simple attitude throughout the calamity. She had a large steel cupboard at her home, as did Gertrude. She assumed the books in those two cupboards were the only ones left.

"She was quite prepared to think the books had come to an end," Kathleen said. Biddy's attitude was simple: "We'll just get rid of what we've got here and see what God wants to happen next."[12] If God wanted the work to continue, it would.

"All my life my mother . . . never for half a second questioned what God allowed to happen, ever," Kathleen said of Biddy's unflappable faith. "She might have been puzzled, but was unperturbed and never desperate."[13] She believed God would be there in the middle of the situation, beside her, no matter what happened.

The OCPA wrangled with insurance claims and paper rationing throughout the war. Lockhart arranged for the books still sitting in Butler and Tanner's warehouse to be moved to his family's business in Dunstable. Several cases went to Gertrude in Dulwich, and even Mary Riley stored some in St. John's Wood. Printing plates turned up at a printing house, and copies of the books in obscure bookstores.

They were still in business.

By mid-war, Biddy proposed printing the revised edition of *Baffled to Fight Better* into the *BTC Monthly Journal*, noting they could simply reprint it into book form when the paper emergency ended. Above all, the OCPA made sure to keep copies of *My Utmost for His Highest* in print.

Demand for all books grew as the war dragged on; people stayed home to read at night, or took a book into the air raid shelters. Raw materials, however, remained in short supply, and paper rationing meant publishers could produce few new titles. The men who actually performed the printing work were leaving the industry for the military, and in December 1941 the British government further reduced publishers' paper rations to 37.5 percent of their prewar usage.[14]

In 1942, the British government printed an important pamphlet: *War Economy Agreement Governing the Printing of Books*. Basically, if the OCPA agreed to a specific set of publishing requirements (margin width, type size, amount of text on a page), the government would increase their paper ration by 50 percent. The books might not look as attractive, but larger numbers could be produced.

They agreed to place a standard publisher's colophon—comparable to a logo—on the back of the title page stating "book production war economy standard," to explain the less attractive appearance and paper quality. With the extra paper ration, the OCPA could reprint all the books destroyed on December 29 except for *The Place of Help*, *Biblical Psychology* outlines, and *Called of God*.[15]

Biddy probably laughed. God could still use Oswald's teachings and he wanted her to continue producing books. Indeed, once it became clear OCPA would remain financially solvent, the committee voted to pay Biddy and Gertrude modest salaries for their work (£220 in 1944 converts to about US $10,000, 2014),[16] along with raising Biddy's entertainment allowance.

She continued to keep her house open as always. Nurses still slept on the floor and guests flocked to 29 Woodberry Crescent. Sunday evenings after the local evening service, Kathleen and her friends gathered around the piano to sing. Biddy loved the evening hymns, particularly "The Day Thou Gavest, Lord, Is Ended."

One night Kathleen's friends Sheila and Rita called and asked to speak with Biddy. Kathleen handed her mother the phone.

Biddy listened. "Well, all right, bring them up here."

"Bring who up here?" Kathleen asked.

Kathleen's friends had met several Yanks in Piccadilly (an entertainment area of London), Biddy explained. "They didn't know what to do with them, so I told the girls to bring them here." She, of course, understood soldiers very well.

The soldiers were in London on leave, "the nicest couple of kids you've ever seen," Kathleen said.

The young people pushed back the table and spent the evening dancing in Biddy's parlor. They enjoyed themselves so much the soldiers returned every evening for the whole fortnight of their leave! "They thought she was the top brick off the chimney," Kathleen laughed. On their final evening, they made a meal to demonstrate their thanks for Biddy, Kathleen, and their young women friends.

Several weeks later Biddy received letters from the soldiers' parents confessing their worry the young men would get in trouble and how thankful they were for her hospitality.[17]

Biddy welcomed everyone who found their way to her door. She often befriended people who came looking for information about Oswald or to purchase one of the books. For example, two weeks after D-Day in 1944, a young man named Daniel Day stopped in, "with some trepidation," to purchase a book for his father's birthday the next day, he hoped. "What a blessing to myself and to many others was to come from that visit," he recalled.[18]

From Biddy he learned of the West China Evangelistic Band, a group led by Vyvyan and Gladys Donnithorne, who were now resettled in Hong Kong after fleeing the revolution in mainland China. Eventually he met the Donnithornes and, much like Vyvyan in his youth, Day felt a tug on his heart to serve as a missionary in China—which he eventually did.

Oswald's books found their way around the globe during the war, some smuggled into Germany, others sent to POW camps. Translations into foreign languages continued, and American publishers produced a number of the books.

In a 1945 *BTC Monthly Journal*, Biddy wrote of her thanks to God for sales and the interest in the books remaining high despite the war, explaining, "The financial position is very satisfactory."[19] Letters regularly arrived from people all over the world, testifying to the spiritual help and guidance they received from the books. People visited her, she sent out books, lives changed.

Euphoria reigned at the end of the war in 1945, and the future looked promising.

# 17

# Yes—But . . . !

## *1946–60*

Trust entirely in God, and when He brings you to the venture,
see that you take it.[1]

*U*nfortunately, like a generation before, war's end did not
bring prosperity to England. Bread rationing remained in
place until 1948 and new clothing was rationed until 1949. Sugar
rationing only ended in 1953. Meat and any other rationed food
supplies finally became available for sale without coupons in June
1954.

When writer Farley Mowat visited London in 1951, the area
around St. Paul's Cathedral shocked him. The former warehouse
lots stretched in all directions, empty bombed-out wastelands of
weeds, grass, and trees. A taxi driver told him the lots under the
ruins, ten years old by then, were too valuable and buyers couldn't
afford to purchase them.[2] Worshipers, however, still visited the
cathedral.

Paper, fortunately, was available in good supply once the war ended, and the OCPA arranged to reprint all the Oswald Chambers books. Biddy compiled two books in 1946: *He Shall Glorify Me*, which focused on the work of the Holy Spirit, and *Approved Unto God*, which included practical studies for young people struggling with what they believed.

She may have decided to produce *Approved Unto God* because young family members leaned away from God into agnosticism during these years. While they adored her, several great-nephews often visited to argue vigorously against her beliefs in God. Biddy, of course, didn't debate, believing the Holy Spirit—particularly through Oswald's books—could speak to them more effectively than she could.

Interest in *My Utmost for His Highest* flourished in the post-war world. The OCPA oversaw editions translated into Braille, Russian, Romanian, Swedish, and even Arabic; ultimately forty different languages in all. Biddy felt gratified when the dean of Westminster Abbey wrote for permission to include quotations from the devotional in the quarterly sent out from the abbey. The Church of England had rarely requested Oswald's material before.

The committee continued its donations, usually prompted by Biddy or Gertrude. They sent gifts to Mrs. Lettie Cowman in America (of *Streams in the Desert*), Lebanon Bible College in Scotland (Biddy's name appeared on marketing materials as secretary, though it appears to have been an honorary position), the House of Praise in India, Spezia Mission in Italy, and the West China Evangelical Society, for which she also served as honorary secretary. The Donnithornes worked with the poorest of the poor in Hong Kong.

As the years went by, her longtime friends began to show their age. Percy and Dais both resigned from the OCPA in late 1949, citing ill health. Gertrude withdrew from several incidental jobs within the committee, as she, too, could not physically manage the tasks any longer.

Biddy still transcribed and compiled, writing to a friend, "The books go out all the time and God still blesses the messages. A new one is being printed, *Conformed to His Image*, and I believe it will prove as good as any of them."[3] *Conformed to His Image* focused on the need for Christians to exercise a disciplined mind and also included a discussion of the psychology of faith.

She repackaged various leaflets and pamphlets into complete books, updated others, and prepared the monthly messages for the *BTC Monthly Journal*. As she finished mining the lectures from the BTC, she began to use talks from Zeitoun. It stirred nostalgia, as she wrote:

> I wish that while transcribing the actual messages I could at the same time reproduce the setting—the little mat hut in the desert; outside—the beauty of the Eastern sky; inside—the gathering of men drawn from very varied callings in life and with as great a variety of views, but met together by a common need of finding Reality.[4]

That many of them did find the Reality for which they sought made those hours, night by night, a wonderful experience, and that tiny place out in the desert where men turned aside became a hallowed spot as God spoke to them.

"You will never know," a former soldier wrote to Biddy, "how many lives were changed as they sat and listened, perhaps for one night only, and then back up the line. My life was changed."[5]

But as Biddy looked at the calendar and her notebooks, it became clear that after twenty years of monthly and bimonthly publication, the *BTC Monthly Journal* had run its course. Most of the material had been published into books; subscriptions had dwindled to five hundred. With eighty-year-old Gertrude's strength ebbing, and Biddy herself nearly seventy years old, it seemed a good time to end the journal. As she wrote to Eva in 1951, "I'm finding the last journal difficult to shape, but begin to see light, odd to think it is the last."[6]

On the twentieth anniversary of its first edition, Gertrude mailed the final *BTC Monthly Journal* to subscribers. As David Lambert wrote in his concluding remarks in the journal, "It has meant a ministry of prayer—without ceasing. It has meant loyal cooperation of willing workers—to mention only his sister, Miss Gertrude Chambers. And it has meant the shining of the light in the hearts of men—'to give the light of the knowledge of the glory of God in the face of Jesus Christ' (2 Cor. 4:6)."[7]

One ministry ended, but others continued. Biddy still received dozens of letters every day in her "Mrs. Oswald Chambers, London," mail slot and typed answers to them all.

In her letters, she answered theological questions concerning Oswald's beliefs, passed on pertinent Scripture passages, and made reading suggestions from the published works. Mail came from everywhere in the world, and she particularly liked to write to lonely missionaries and package up books to send them with her letters. The book parcels regularly spanned the globe, sent as far as Dohnavur Fellowship in India for missionary Amy Carmichael, the Gobi Desert for the China Inland Mission, and to fledgling Christian bookstores in Africa.

Her ministry of interruptions and hospitality continued unabated. When new families moved into the neighborhood, Biddy brought a welcome offering she baked herself. Neighbors with personal problems often visited for advice. "She sort of looked after everybody," Kathleen said.[8]

One of her neighbors, Mrs. Ball, remembered stepping through the side door (which was never locked)—"like everybody did," Kathleen remembered—and seeing Biddy at work. Biddy stopped typing immediately and made a cup of tea. Like her husband and her God, she gave each person her undivided attention.

One day a distraught woman who had left her husband visited; she didn't know what God wanted her to do next.

"Do you know where to go tomorrow and this weekend?" Biddy asked.

She nodded.

"Well, if God's given you somewhere to go this weekend and tomorrow, then he'll arrange where you're going to go for the rest of your life. So you've nothing to worry about. We'll just pray and commit it to God."

On hearing Kathleen tell the story, Mrs. Ball thought Biddy's response came from something she had done "so many times herself in her own experience. It was all right."[9]

Biddy led Bible studies and discussions of Oswald's books twice a week, with up to fifty people in attendance. Kathleen's friends often dropped by to visit with Biddy. "All my friends had their own homes, mind you, but they all seemed to come here, want to get married from here, have their babies here."[10]

Kathleen frequently returned home to find strangers comfortably ensconced in the kitchen. They'd greet her with, "We've been here all day and your mother told us to stay for supper, so we're trying to find the things to lay the table."[11]

One day Kathleen shook her head over an unusual group of surprise dinner guests, wondering how they could possibly get along. Biddy remarked, "We told God so we can laugh about it, and it will be very interesting to see what happens."[12]

Kathleen never married, and while she loved children, she never raised any of her own. After World War II, she worked with handicapped children as the secretary in a five-hundred-student school. She taught Bible classes and led girls' clubs. She owned a car and often took her mother into London for entertainment. Biddy loved to ride in the car and, like the risk-taker she always was, urged her daughter to drive faster. "We had a very good relationship," Kathleen said. "I could tell her anything."[13]

The household expanded in 1947 when Miss Ashe, eighty-three years old, finally returned from Cairo. Always a challenging woman, she spent long hours examining the newspaper, her creative mind fixated on intellectual pursuits and solving crimes for Scotland Yard. Eventually Miss Ashe recognized she wasn't functioning up to her usual abilities and felt only relief when Biddy and Kathleen moved her to an Eastbourne nursing asylum in 1951.

Biddy and Kathleen visited Miss Ashe regularly until she died in April 1956—undoubtedly pleased to enter the gates of heaven. BTC friend Reverend Philip Hancock (pastor at St. Andrew's Presbyterian Church in Middlesex) signed the death certificate and arranged to have the retired social worker's body cremated—a common arrangement for a penniless spinster who had outlived her family.[14]

The 1950s marked the end of many close friendships on earth: Oswald's sister Bertha and the EGM's George Swan (retired to Middlesex) died in 1951. Dais became a widow at Percy Lockhart's death in 1952. Jimmy Hanson and Mary Riley both died in the spring of 1956.

Biddy carried on. She regularly visited a podiatrist and suffered from deafness in one ear. From time to time, she hired a secretary to take dictation and opened her home to live-in house girls, usually from abroad, to help with the rough cleaning chores. Kathleen insisted they take a weeklong holiday to the sea each year—which Biddy loved.

"She would be completely content, when we did have holidays, to go down to Cornwall on the end of the rocks and sit there all day long," Kathleen said. "We'd go out about 4 am with the fishermen to catch fish."[15]

Mother and daughter lived companionably together, working on jigsaw puzzles, reading, and enjoying their dog; Simon was one of many. "She adored animals," Kathleen said.[16] In addition, Kathleen often knit items for the children she worked with.

Once a week, at noon, Biddy walked to nearby St. James Church to hear the midday organ recital. She read *The Daily Telegraph* every day and devoured all of Winston Churchill's war books. Biddy still enjoyed concerts in London and each year visited the

Art Academy for the exhibition of new portraits and landscapes.[17] She loved to window-shop and go out for lunch or tea.

Biddy regularly corresponded with Eva, and in one letter described entertaining sixty people—which she noted was quite a lot to look after! Eva and Stephen lived in the vicarage at Ross-on-Wye, a Herefordshire market town near the Welsh border. Her grandson later described Eva as being "like a Bible concordance; she was phenomenally well read. She wore out Bibles."[18]

Eva's son observed his mother "always quoted the lovely and powerful thoughts of *My Utmost for His Highest*. She found strength, courage and comfort from the writings of OC." She and Biddy enjoyed their visits with one another over the years.[19]

Biddy also relished Gladys Ingram Donnithorne's rare furloughs to England from Hong Kong and remained in contact with the Hancocks.

One fall day in the mid-1950s, Biddy received a letter from a Dutchman attending the World Evangelization Crusade School in Scotland. During a period of convalescence, Andrew van der Bijl had devoured *My Utmost for His Highest* and wanted her to know the great comfort the book had given him. She invited him to visit.[20]

The young man who soon became known as the Bible-smuggling Brother Andrew stayed in the Chambers house for a week that Christmas. They became fast friends, and he later took copies of *My Utmost for His Highest* all over the world through his ministry.

Of his visit, Brother Andrew remembered Biddy's warmth and generosity, along with how her neighbors saw the woman who walked to the post office to mail Oswald's books around the world: they likened her to Enoch, who walked with God.

# 18

## Undaunted Radiance

### 1961–66

Nothing can wedge in between the love of God and the saint.[1]

*I*n a perfect story, Biddy Chambers would have reached the final scribble of shorthand on the last page of the concluding notebook and transcribed it into her typewriter. She would have struck the period key for the bottom row right and tugged the paper from the machine.

Setting it on the last stack of Oswald's transcribed words, Biddy would have picked up her worn Bible and a framed photograph of Oswald and gone into her bedroom. She'd know Kathleen would find her the next morning, hands across the Bible and photograph on her chest, eyes closed with a smile on her lips as she slept in Christ.

When Biddy next opened her eyes, Jesus would greet her with warm words: "Well done, good and faithful servant. Enter into your rest."

Looking past him, she would see the first greeter: Oswald.

Joy.

Rest.

Heaven.

But Biddy's story didn't end that way. Biddy had one last challenge before her welcome home.

Age catches up with everyone, and as Biddy neared her eightieth birthday, her loved ones died. Second only to Biddy in devotion to Oswald, Gertrude Chambers's health faltered in the 1950s and the family placed her in a nursing home. She died there in August 1960 at the age of eighty-seven; her death certificate listed her profession as "secretary to a publishing house."

Biddy's brother, Bert, died in September 1963. Six months later Dais, her closest confidante, died in Dunstable at the age of eighty-four.

By then, Biddy's own health had spiraled down.

In 1961 she began having mental difficulties never fully explained. With only a few of her shorthand notes still unpublished—the incomplete Ezekiel, Isaiah, and Jeremiah lectures—she concentrated on compiling an updated version of *Seed Thoughts Calendar*. She only managed the first three months before it became clear she would not be able to finish.

As Kathleen wrote, "Towards the end of my mother's life, God allowed her to become very ill with a mental illness (not senility) and her mind became clouded and tormented. She received treatment and became restored for nearly a year, before the illness returned to stay until she went into God's presence."[2]

One close friend described the suffering woman as not having Alzheimer's but she "wasn't Auntie Biddy either."[3] OCPA members noted her personality change; no longer calm and serene, Biddy often acted agitated and fearful.[4]

Kathleen quit her job to care for her mother. "It was a strange time," Kathleen said. "It was difficult for her and it was difficult for me and it was completely inexplicable why she was ill the way she was. It was a dark time for her."[5]

Biddy still found solace in the psalms and the *Daily Light*, which Kathleen read aloud each day. One morning Kathleen read a forgotten passage from Isaiah 32:17: "the effect of righteousness [shall be] quietness and assurance forever."

Biddy seized the verse, Kathleen said, "something she felt strong to hold onto for such a long time."[6] Despite her ailment, Biddy scrawled a birthday greeting for her daughter in 1963, reminding her, as she had every year, of how precious Kathleen was. "God bless you honey in 1963, every day of it. I can be grateful enough for all you have meant to me this whole year."[7]

In spite of her illness, eventually listed as "uremia and chronic nephritis," or kidney disease along with arteriosclerosis (hardening of the arteries), Biddy still attended the OCPA committee meetings held at Woodberry Crescent, though she seldom participated in the discussions.

However, the October 31, 1964, OCPA minutes shared disappointing news:

> Due to illness, it was noted that for the first time in the history of the association, Mrs. Chambers was unable to be present. Her absence was a challenge to us all to be urgent at the Throne of Grace seeking His Healing hand to be exercised in her behalf in faith that she may be restored to health according to his gracious purpose.[8]

Kathleen was alone with her for most of this time period, but by the end had to put her mother into a nursing home. The OCPA eventually paid all the bills, which included full-time nursing the last year.

Throughout her life Biddy believed nothing transpired without God's knowledge. Certainly her salvation was never at risk, even if her difficulties challenged her faith and that of her loved ones. A person's mental capacity or sickness has no bearing on God's love and acceptance of them.

Forty-nine years and two months after her husband's death, Biddy died with Kathleen by her side on January 15, 1966. She was eighty-two years old.

At Christmas in 1920, Biddy had written in her diary, "Lord, Jesus, I give me to you. This life is one of learning and thinking. In heaven we shall see what we have been thinking about."[9]

Biddy had sent a letter to Eva in February 1939 referring to a friend but voicing her own confidence in God at life's end. Eva transcribed Biddy's letter into her diary as comfort on the day she got news of her old friend's death: "I have been reading 2 Corinthians 5 today with [their friend] especially in mind . . . full of pain and it can't be long I think, before she is absent from it. I felt the 'therefore' was such a wonderful word. The 'yet' always outweighs the thought."[10]

> Though we have known Christ after the flesh, yet now henceforth know we him no more. Therefore if any man be in Christ, he is a new creature: old things are passed away; behold, all things are become new. (2 Cor. 5:16–17)

On that January 15, 1966, Eva added two Bible passages in addition to quoting the 1939 letter. She drew comfort from Nehemiah 9:12, "Thou leddest them . . . to give them light in the way wherein they should go," and Jeremiah 31:13, "I will turn their mourning into joy, and will comfort them."

Despite rarely writing in her diaries, every January 15, for years, Eva wrote, "B. C. in his presence 1966." She included Bible verses and quotations, still grieving and missing her friend. Kathleen gave Eva two books Biddy had owned: *Psychology of Redemption* and *Diary of an Old Soul*.[11] "Oh, Lord God, Thou knowest my gratitude," Eva wrote in the diary.

At Kathleen's direction, Biddy's body was cremated, and family and friends held a small service a few days later, January 20, at St. Marylebone Crematorium. Her ashes were spread in the Willow Gardens, a tranquil spot at the crematorium near Hampstead Heath.[12]

As Kathleen later wrote Eva, "It's so very strange to realize she's not here anymore. Death is *so* final, the beginning of something magnificent and new, but also the end of something known and loved and seen."[13]

Kathleen placed a bench in her honor at nearby Hampstead Heath, where Biddy liked to walk. She took her mother's place on the OCPA committee and lived the rest of her life sending out books, writing letters to missionaries, entertaining journalists, answering innumerable questions, and "behaving just as radical as her father," according to Brother Andrew.[14]

Author Os Guinness, nephew of the Swedish translator of *My Utmost for His Highest*, Joy Guinness, met Kathleen once after a speaking engagement.

> She came up out of the crowd and said, "I hear you were named after my father. How do you like the name?" I told her that I admired her father enormously, and often read him, but had to admit that I did not like the name. She laughed, and said, "He hated it too!" (Which actually made it better for me.)[15]

Kathleen was opinionated but very polite, and never went without offering a cup of tea and cake for visitors. She cooked meals for the OCPA meetings held at her home and supported missionaries around the world, continuing her mother's legacy. Brother Andrew remembered her providing copies of *My Utmost for His Highest* for him to take behind the Iron Curtain.

When asked once about Oswald, she said, "I would have liked to have known my father, but I never did."[16] While Kathleen certainly had heard a great deal about him from her mother and friends, she didn't really remember him herself.

Kathleen Marian Chambers died on May 30, 1997, at the age of eighty-four. She, too, was cremated and her ashes scattered at the Willow Gardens, though her funeral was held at Muswell Hill Baptist Church on June 11, 1997. Reverend Michael Caddick from the church gathered her friends "to remember and celebrate Kathleen's life." A brief service of committal followed at St. Marylebone Crematorium and then her friends met at a local hotel for refreshments.

The OCPA, now known as The Oswald Chambers Publication Association, Limited, continues to oversee publication of Oswald Chambers's books.

Perhaps the final word on the Beloved Disciple who served her God and her husband's teaching about God so very well belongs to a man who came to faith as a result of Oswald Chambers and the books Biddy compiled.

A soldier who avoided all the BTC folks at Zeitoun when he served in the British Army, Stephen Pulford found the love of his life and his eternity as a result of the Holy Spirit–led couple. A rector with the Church of England, the Reverend Pulford wrote Biddy's obituary for *The Life of Faith* magazine on February 17, 1966, in which he noted:

> It was during the Palestine campaign I learnt of Mr. Chambers' death. And although from the human point of view his passing seemed an irreparable loss, it marked the beginning of a ministry which he might never have achieved had he lived to pursue it. And this is where the slow-moving miracle (as we count time) begins.[17]

He described Biddy's astonishing shorthand skill and dedication to the books, while paying tribute to the importance of Oswald Chambers's books in the lives of so many—including his own.

Stephen Pulford ended with a romantic flourish:

The ocean now separates the earthly remains of this devoted pair, but they are both in the presence of the Lord, and of no two saints may it more truthfully be said, "Their works do follow them."[18]

What kind of woman married Oswald Chambers?

A woman who trained to be the prime minister's secretary but chose a different master, Gertrude Annie Hobbs Chambers lived her life to the utmost for God's highest purposes, just as she and Oswald pledged all those years ago at St. Paul's Cathedral.

To Biddy and Oswald, glory always belonged to God.

## The End

# Acknowledgments

Writing *Mrs. Oswald Chambers* has been a joy, delight, and honor. I've been led by God from the very beginning and I'm astounded at the help I received along the way—often from strangers. It has been a walk of faith, as I've prayed a daily reminder, "This is your book, Lord; I am your hands, fingers, and mind. Use it to your glory." People who prayed for me have been of great encouragement.

I begin my thanks with David McCasland and his biography *Oswald Chambers: Abandoned for God*, the reading of which started me on this journey. He has been gracious, helpful, and encouraging throughout the years I've been immersed in the life and work of Oswald and Biddy Chambers.

My quest began on a day my agent and I planned to discuss what I should write next. Before we got to that conversation, an editor called asking for an inspirational novel set in World War I. I said, "What about the Oswald Chambers story? He led a revival in Egypt during WWI." The idea changed the course of my writing and personal life. Janet Kobobel Grant, my agent and friend, provided wise counsel and encouragement from that day on. I could not have produced this book without her.

Wheaton College's Special Collections Library holds the Oswald Chambers papers—many of which are McCasland's research from writing *Abandoned for God*. Archivist Keith Call has been a source of generous support and help throughout. His colleagues also assisted me and stood by—perhaps praying—when, after two straight days of scanning documents, my scanner died and this technology-challenged writer had to buy and set up a new one!

With typical spiritual acumen, author Robin Jones Gunn introduced me to her friend Nicholas Gray—who was only available for lunch on the one full day I spent in Scotland researching the aforementioned novel. A member of the Oswald Chambers Publications Association, Nicholas suggested I might someday write a biography of Biddy Chambers. I laughed, but the idea burrowed into my soul. He was the first person to suggest I needed prayer support—which was true. I'm grateful for his encouragement.

Peter Wenham of Australia sent me an email the day after I wrote about Oswald Chambers's death in my novel. His subject line: "looking for information about Oswald Chambers in Egypt." His grandfather had attended Oswald's burial service, and he had photos we had never seen before. He and his wife, Meredith, also sent me ninety-seven pages of information from their visit to the Cadbury Research Library's Special Collections at the University of Birmingham in the UK—which proved invaluable in the writing of *Mrs. Oswald Chambers*. Thank you, Peter and Meredith; thank you, also, Cadbury Research Library and Ken Montgomery of the YMCA, UK.

Thanks to Dr. Ken Boa and the good folks at Breakpoint.com who provided the Great Books CD series. We have listened to *Themes in My Utmost for His Highest* countless times.

It took a while to track down Brother Andrew, one of the few people still alive who had known Biddy Chambers. My thanks to him and to Os Guinness for answering questions.

A surprise interview with Eva Spink Pulford's grandson Reverend Christopher Pulford at the very end blessed me tremendously.

Christopher hunted up photos and set up an interview with his father, Eva's son Canon Ian Pulford—who met Biddy as a child. I thought the book was done and then I had the opportunity to talk with someone who had met Biddy!

I'm astonished at the primary source material available on Ancestry .com and the willingness of family members both to talk to a biographer and to share photos and correspondence: Keith Moore, Judy Bolter-Smith, and Audrey Donnithorne—Gladys's daughter.

And who can forget Google?

Others who deserve nods for information, advice, or beta reading include Amanda Sorenson, Linda Livingstone, Jo Miller, Rachel Durham, Wendy Hinman, Marianne Campbell, Cathy LaGrow, Jed Macosko, Mary and Brian Keeley, Rachel Kent, Wendy Lawton, Rachelle Gardner, and all my Wandering View friends.

This biography wouldn't be in your hands without the Baker Books staff, primarily my editor Rebekah Guzman, as well as Lindsey Spoolstra, Michelle Bardin, Collette Kischner, Patti Brinks, and Abby Van Wormer. Additional thanks to Jamie Clarke Chavez and my writer friends at Books & Such Literary Agency. Acknowledgment goes to Glenn Gohr, my fifth cousin twice removed and genealogy colleague, who twenty years ago admonished me, "You're a fine researcher and writer, Michelle, but you need to document your work." He was right.

Gratitude must be extended to my assistant, Leah Campbell Warren, who discussed every chapter, draft, and idea. She also analyzed *My Utmost for His Highest* readings for the insight in this biography. Great job, Leah.

Final thanks go to my family: I could not have written my books, nor lived my life with grace and joy, without all of you. My wonderful husband, Robert, sat through innumerable discussions of the books, publishing, Oswald and Biddy, and what should we have for dinner? He's been my support, my patron of the arts, my travel companion, and my happiness for most of my life. I may not be as poetic as Oswald, but I love you, Robert.

Thank you, readers. May this book open your hearts and minds to a God who loves you with an everlasting love. I'm with Oswald— I desire this book to be nothing more than a footnote in your relationship with Jesus.

*Soli Deo Gloria.*

Michelle Ule
Northern California, fall 2017

# Appendix

### Biddy Chambers and the Writing of
### My Utmost for His Highest, 1924–27

When Biddy descended the narrow basement stairs each morning after completing her household chores, she entered an office stuffed with boxes, books, a table, a Royal typewriter, and many notebooks filled with her shorthand notes from Oswald's lectures.

In 1924, Biddy decided to expand the idea behind the *Seed Thoughts Calendar*, published in 1919 Egypt, into a devotional book. For most readers, daily devotionals served as spiritual aids to prompt prayer and meditation on specific Bible passages.

She was familiar with the *Daily Light* and Charles Spurgeon's three devotionals. Biddy would have turned the pages of Lettie Cowan's 1925 *Streams in the Desert* devotional with interest when she received a copy. These devotionals all may have played a role in how she envisioned her new book.

Writing a devotional is a daunting task. While intimately familiar with Oswald's words and concepts, Biddy's work to put together 366 devotional readings of about 250 words each required a great deal of prayer, thought, and time.

She worked alone. No one reviewed the notes with her, debated the merits of a passage or theme, or even discussed if the chosen excerpts made sense. She relied upon the Holy Spirit to direct her as she paged through her notes.

Biddy often chose passages for a single devotion from as many as three or four different lectures. One paragraph may have sparked a memory of a similar idea from another talk. Perhaps she remembered exhausted soldiers in a sandy hut responding to something Oswald said that reminded her of neat BTC students scribbling at desks. A lecture given in rainy Blackpool may have paralleled the easy familiarity of a BTC devotion hour discussion. She pieced together a crazy quilt of concepts into a beautiful work of practical spiritual warmth.

The words and original concepts may have been Oswald's, but the potency of *My Utmost for His Highest* really came from Biddy's Holy Spirit–inspired editorial skill.

Dr. Jed Macosko, coauthor of *The Daily Companion Guide to My Utmost for His Highest*, didn't discern an overall pattern to why she assigned readings to a particular date. He suspected Biddy may have typed up the devotionals, anchored the personal ones to their calendar dates, and fit the rest into a more haphazard order.

"She may have worried if she compiled all the devotionals on the theme of, say, brokenness in the month of April, it might have been too much for the reader," he said. "So she spaced them—two in a row, then something different."

With one typed devotion filling each page, she could "easily shuffle the pile and make them random," he said.

Macosko pointed out many of the snippets come from Oswald's 1915 *Studies in the Sermon on the Mount*, rereleased in a fourth edition in 1929. "It would take a long time to go through the stacks of notebooks, read her shorthand, decide which were good and then type them up." Macosko added that, in the final analysis, "Biddy took the cream of the crop from Oswald's work and that's why *My Utmost for His Highest* is so powerful."[1]

In her dedication to the students of the BTC, Biddy said the readings were chiefly taken from the BTC lectures and the nightly talks at Zeitoun, while a number are also from the BTC's devotional hour.

The devotional hour was reserved for Oswald's full-time, live-in students once a week, and "many of the students marked [it as] an epoch in their life with God."[2] Oswald used the hour to discuss heart issues and answer their individual spiritual questions. He probed their souls, with special attention given to those students desiring to serve in the mission field.

Biddy may have sought lecture quotes of Oswald's "signature" themes to amplify them in *My Utmost for His Highest*. Dr. Ken Boa identified at least sixteen major themes in *My Utmost for His Highest*.[3] They are:

1. A surrender of the will and the cost of discipleship

2. Intimacy with Christ and holy aspiration

3. Identification with Christ

4. Abiding in Christ

5. Prayer

6. God's guidance in our lives

7. Private communion vs. public activity

8. The role of service

9. Intercession and others-centered ministry

10. Trust and obedience

11. Faithfulness in the ordinary

12. Pleasing God rather than others

13. Self-knowledge

14. The thoughtful life

15. The role of adversity

16. Perspectives on the past and the future

Reviewing this list from the perspective of Biddy's biography, it is easy to see Boa's themes reflected in her post-Oswald life. She relied on prayer to follow God's hand in her daily activities and to direct her, Kathleen, and the book publishing enterprise. The lessons she learned from the severe mercy of Oswald's death were central to her relationship with God and her life ministry that followed. These themes may very well have instigated the pointed devotionals in *My Utmost for His Highest*.

Oswald did not mince words; neither did Biddy.

Oswald and Biddy saw their BTC calling as preparing men and women for life in the mission field. They viewed Zeitoun as an opportunity to experience missionary life firsthand for future training purposes. For that reason, many of Oswald's books and the devotionals in *My Utmost for His Highest* describe the spiritual fortitude required for missionary life.

As all followers of Jesus Christ are called to proclaim the good news, *My Utmost for His Highest* applies to Christians across generations—no matter where they live or serve.

So how did Biddy choose what went where?

Devotional writers are conscious of the calendar—what happened on specific dates. Most tailor particular devotions for specific dates to begin with: holidays like Christmas serve as an anchor for placement.

In the case of *My Utmost for His Highest*, the Christmas reading looks at the traditional quote from Isaiah 7:14: "Behold, a virgin shall bring forth a son, and they shall call His name Emmanuel, which being interpreted is, God with us."

Biddy's first title, "Let Us Keep to the Point," on January 1 begins the devotional by reminding readers the point of Christians' lives is to surrender their will to Jesus absolutely and irrevocably. It's always helpful to begin a new year with priorities in place.

As indicated earlier, an examination of Chambers family dates—Biddy's and Oswald's birthdays, their wedding day, and the shattering date of his death—indicates she may have specifically assigned messages to them. Other family dates, such as Kathleen's and Dais's birthdays, as well as the death of her father, contain no obvious correlation.

Perhaps the final statement on December 31 sums up the BTC—better things to come—element of Biddy's life and serves as a clarion call to readers: "Let the past sleep, but let it sleep on the bosom of Christ. Leave the Irreparable Past in His hands, and step out into the Irresistible Future with Him."

We can do no less.

# *Notes*

### Prologue: Faith and Experience

1. Oswald Chambers, *My Utmost for His Highest*, classic edition (Uhrichsville, OH: Barbour Publishing, 1963), November 13; www.utmost.org.

2. David McCasland, *Oswald Chambers: Abandoned to God* (Grand Rapids: Discovery House, 1993), 167.

3. Ibid., 150.

### Chapter 1 Discovering Divine Designs

1. Chambers, *My Utmost for His Highest*, November 14.

2. "Death Certificate Samuel Hobbs," Wheaton College Special Collections Library (SC/122), Chambers papers, series 1, box 10, folder 17. Unless otherwise noted, all quoted material from Chambers papers is from series 1 (Oswald Chambers).

3. William R. Smith, "Woolwich 1895 (Report of the Medical Officer of Health for Woolwich)," *London's Pulse: Medical Office of Health Reports 1848–1972*, accessed March 8, 2016, http://wellcomelibrary.org/moh/report/b1982323x#?c=0&m=0&s=0&cv=0.

4. "Death Certificate Samuel Hobbs."

5. "Kathleen Chambers Interview by David McCasland, September 1991," Wheaton College Special Collections Library (SC/122), Chambers papers, box 10, folder 23, unpaginated transcription.

6. Physical descriptions come from photos and 1908 US immigration papers (Ancestry.com); see "New York Passenger Lists 1820–1956 Roll T715, Roll 1109."

7. "Gardner's Bankruptcy," *The Jurist* vol. IX, no. 429 (March 29, 1845), http://heinonline.org/HOL/LandingPage?handle=hein.journals/jurlonos9&div=18&id=&page=.

8. 1871 census on church job; auctioneer and elopement from examination of marriage certificate, along with that of Emily's brother Herbert three days later at same place far from anyone's home in Canterbury. All the material comes from Ancestry.com in the Chambers family tree compiled by the author: http://trees .ancestry.com/tree/80748053/family.

9. "Henry Hobbs Probate Report, 1898," *National Probate Calendar (Index of Wills and Administrations), 1858–1966* (England & Wales).

10. Jerome B. Howard, ed., "An English Idea of 'The Typewriter Girl,'" *Phonographic Magazine* vol. 9 (January 15, 1895): 25, http://bit.ly/2jCu3wU.

11. Ibid.

12. "History of Eltham," *Ideal Homes: A History of South-east London Suburbs*, accessed March 6, 2017, http://www.ideal-homes.org.uk/greenwich/assets /histories/eltham.

13. "Eltham Park Baptist Church Records and Minutes," Wheaton College Special Collections Library (SC/122), Chambers papers, box 6, folder 2.

14. Ibid.

15. Ibid.

16. "Kathleen Chambers Interview by David McCasland."

17. Reverend Maurice Winterburn, *The League of Prayer: An Historical Review 1891–1991*, Wheaton College Special Collections Library (SC/122), Chambers papers, box 6, folder 6.

## Chapter 2 The Spontaneity of Love

1. Chambers, *My Utmost for His Highest*, April 30.

2. "Inflation Calculator," http://www.in2013dollars.com/1908-dollars-to -2016-dollars.

3. The generally accepted speed noted in McCasland, *Abandoned to God*, 146. Other writers, including Kathleen Chambers, suggest shorthand speed ranged from 150–275.

4. McCasland, *Abandoned to God*, 151.

5. "Kathleen Chambers Interview by David McCasland."

6. McCasland, *Abandoned to God*, 149.

7. Ibid.

8. Ibid., 151.

## Chapter 3 The Secret of the Lord

1. Chambers, *My Utmost for His Highest*, June 3.

2. B. Chambers, *Oswald Chambers: His Life and Work*, first edition (London: OCPA, 1933), 120.

3. Born in 1865, Ireland. Age from her death certificate; see Chambers papers, box 10, folder 17, along with references in Ancestry.com immigration forms.

4. Chambers, *Oswald Chambers: His Life and Work*, first edition, 154.

5. McCasland, *Abandoned to God*, 157.

6. Ibid., 154.

7. "Mrs. Hobbs Correspondence, Undated Letter," Wheaton College Special Collections Library (SC/122), Chambers papers, box 6, folder 9.

8. McCasland, "Letter to Biddy, April 13, 1909," *Abandoned to God*, 166.

9. "Kathleen Chambers Interview by David McCasland."

10. McCasland, *Abandoned to God*, 169.

11. Ibid., 159.

12. Ibid., 171.

13. Oswald Chambers, "The Servant as His Lord," *The Complete Works of Oswald Chambers* (Grand Rapids: Discovery House, 2000), 1280.

14. Ibid., "Not Knowing Whither," 881.

15. McCasland, *Abandoned to God*, 174.

16. "Letter to Gladys Ingram, Oct. 17, 1915," Wheaton College Special Collections Library (SC/122), Chambers papers, box 1, folder 1.

17. Computations taken from MeasuringWorth.com, https://www.measuring worth.com/calculators/exchange/result_exchange.php.

18. "Oswald Letter to Emily Hobbs, May 1910," Wheaton College Special Collections Library (SC/122), Chambers papers, box 4, folder 14.

19. "Christine Reynolds Information," Wheaton College Special Collections Library (SC/122), Chambers papers, box 10, folder 19.

## Chapter 4 Building for Eternity

1. Chambers, *My Utmost for His Highest*, May 7.

2. "Dorothy Docking Memories," Wheaton College Special Collections Library (SC/122), Chambers papers, box 11, folder 10.

3. Reverend Theo M. Bamber, "In a Remembrance of Gertrude Chambers," Wheaton College Special Collections Library (SC/122), Chambers papers, box 10, folder 17.

4. "Kathleen Chambers Interview by David McCasland."

5. Ibid.

6. Chambers, *Oswald Chambers: His Life and Work*, first edition, 127.

7. Wheaton College Special Collections Library (SC/122), Chambers papers, box 4, folder 15; descriptions come from *Home and Gardens Magazine*, March 1966.

8. McCasland, *Abandoned to God*, 182.

9. "BTC 1914 Prospectus," Wheaton College Special Collections Library (SC/122), Chambers papers, box 4, folder 15.

10. Ibid.

11. McCasland, *Abandoned to God*, 184.

12. Photograph of the actual sign posted. Wheaton College Special Collections Library (SC/122), Chambers papers, series 5 (photographs), box 37, item 52. Living in a dormitory room for one year cost £40 (about $1600 US 2014); a single room raised the rate to £60 ($2400 US 2014). Biddy never sent away anyone for lack of funds because God always provided what they needed.

13. Chambers, *My Utmost for His Highest*, August 1.

14. *The College*, 22, Wheaton College Special Collections Library (SC/122), Chambers papers, box 4, folder 15.

15. Ibid.; "Kathleen Chambers Interview by David McCasland."

## Chapter 5 Vision

1. Chambers, *My Utmost for His Highest*, March 11.
2. McCasland, *Abandoned to God*, 174.
3. Chambers, *My Utmost for His Highest*, December 13.
4. *The College*, 31.
5. *BTC Monthly Journal*, September 1937, Wheaton College Special Collections Library (SC/122), Chambers papers, box 14, folder 5.
6. McCasland, *Abandoned to God*, 188.
7. *The College*, 40.
8. Chambers, *My Utmost for His Highest*, February 5.
9. *The College*, 11.
10. Louise Lewis, ed., *Fundamentals of Midwifery: A Textbook for Students* (John Wiley & Sons, 2014), http://bit.ly/1L4zUkP.
11. While Chambers's letters and diary entries are sprinkled with these women's nicknames, the author will use their real names for clarity in this biography.
12. Author conversation with Christopher Pulford, Eva Spink Pulford's grandson, October 6, 2016.
13. "A Brief History of the OC Publications," *1940s BTC Monthly Journal*, 71–72, Wheaton College Special Collections Library (SC/122), Chambers papers, box 15.
14. *The College*, 12.
15. McCasland, *Abandoned to God*, 191.
16. Ibid.
17. Chambers, *Oswald Chambers: His Life and Work*, first edition, 197.

## Chapter 6 The Baffling Call of God

1. Chambers, *My Utmost for His Highest*, August 5.
2. Chambers, *Oswald Chambers: His Life and Work*, first edition, 207.
3. Chambers, *My Utmost for His Highest*, February 9.
4. "Kathleen Chambers Interview by David McCasland."
5. Chambers, *My Utmost for His Highest*, February 18.
6. "Kathleen Chambers Interview by David McCasland."
7. *The College*, 12.
8. Ibid.
9. Chambers, *Oswald Chambers: His Life and Work*, third edition (London: Simpkin Marshall, 1959), 158.
10. Ibid.
11. McCasland, *Abandoned to God*, 200.
12. Ibid., 205.
13. Ibid., 206.
14. Chambers, *Oswald Chambers: His Life and Work*, first edition, 264.

## Chapter 7 The Undetected Sacredness of Circumstances

1. Chambers, *My Utmost for His Highest*, November 7.
2. Karl Baedeker, *Egypt and the Sudan: Handbook for Travelers*, seventh edition (Leipzig: 1914), https://archive.org/details/egyptsdnhandookarl.

3. Ibid.

4. "Jessop Letter to Mott 1913," Wheaton College Special Collections Library (SC/122), Chambers papers, box 8, folder 12.

5. William Howard Taft, *Service with Fighting Men* (New York: New York Association Press, 1922), https://archive.org/details/servicewithfight02taft.

6. "Jessop Report, July 26, 1915," Wheaton College Special Collections Library (SC/122), Chambers papers, box 8, folder 12.

7. Ibid.

8. Chambers, *Oswald Chambers: His Life and Work*, third edition, 213.

9. O. E. Burton, *The Auckland Regiment* (Auckland, NZ: Whitcombe and Tombs Ltd., 1922), http://nzetc.victoria.ac.nz/tm/scholarly/tei-WH1Auck-t1 -body-d3.html.

10. Chambers, *Oswald Chambers: His Life and Work*, first edition, 239.

11. Ibid.

12. Ibid., 240.

13. Author email with writer Wendy Hinman, who visited Cairo on a short-term missionary trip in 2015, February 29, 2016.

14. "Oswald Letter to Gladys Ingram, November 5, 1915," Wheaton College Special Collections Library (SC/122), Chambers papers, box 1, folder 1.

15. Computations taken from MeasuringWorth.com, https://www.measuring worth.com/calculators/exchange/result_exchange.php.

16. "Oswald Notes to Biddy, Dec. 7–22, 1915," Wheaton College Special Collections Library (SC/122), Chambers papers, series 2 (Biddy Chambers), box 18, folder 1.

17. David Bilton, "Hull Pals: 10th, 11th, 12th and 13th Battalions East Yorkshire Regiment; South Yorkshire," *Pen and Sword* (2014): 70–74.

## Chapter 8 The Determination to Serve

1. Chambers, *My Utmost for His Highest*, February 23.

2. Chambers, *Oswald Chambers: His Life and Work*, first edition, 273.

3. Chambers, *Oswald Chambers: His Life and Work*, third edition, 238.

4. "Kathleen Chambers Interview by David McCasland."

5. Author email with Marianne Campbell, who traveled to Egypt circa 1980, February 27, 2016.

6. Chambers, *Oswald Chambers: His Life and Work*, first edition, 256.

7. "Spink Letter, January 10, 1916," Wheaton College Special Collections Library (SC/122), Chambers papers, box 9, folder 4.

8. Ibid.

9. Author conversation with Christopher Pulford, October 6, 2016.

10. "Spink Letter, January 10, 1916."

11. Katherine Ashe, "The Book of the Bungalow," in *Oswald Chambers: His Life and Work*, second edition (London: Simpkin Marshall, 1938), 444.

12. Chambers, *Oswald Chambers: His Life and Work*, third edition, 225.

13. Ashe, "The Book of the Bungalow," 425, 432.

14. A. D. Carbery, *The New Zealand Medical Service in the Great War 1914–1918* (Auckland, NZ: Whitcombe and Tombs Ltd., 1924), http://nzetc.victoria.ac .nz/tm/scholarly/tei-WH1-Medi-t1-g1-t1-body-d4.html.

15. Ashe, "The Book of the Bungalow," 436.
16. Chambers, *Oswald Chambers: His Life and Work*, third edition, 226.
17. "Kathleen Chambers Interview by David McCasland."
18. Author conversation with Christopher Pulford, October 6, 2016.
19. Four Ingram siblings married four Donnithorne siblings; Gladys and Vyvyan were the last to wed in 1919. Information about the Donnithorne family came from Gladys's daughter Audrey Donnithorne and niece Judy Bolster-Smith through email with author, March 3, 2016.

## Chapter 9  The Destitution of Service

1. Chambers, *My Utmost for His Highest*, February 25.
2. "Letter to Biddy, June 12, 1916," Wheaton College Special Collections Library (SC/122), Chambers papers, series 2, box 17.
3. Ibid.
4. Ibid.
5. Ashe, "The Book of the Bungalow," 429.
6. Anonymous, *For the Millions of Men Now Under Arms* (YMCA: 1915), https://archive.org/stream/formillionsofmen02newy/formillionsofmen02newy _djvu.txt.
7. Chambers, *Oswald Chambers: His Life and Work*, first edition, 297.
8. Computations taken from MeasuringWorth.com, https://www.measuring worth.com/calculators/exchange/result_exchange.php.
9. *Tongues of Fire*, September 1916, Wheaton College Special Collections Library (SC/122), Chambers papers, box 12, folder 6.
10. "Kathleen Chambers Interview by David McCasland."
11. Chambers, *Oswald Chambers: His Life and Work*, first edition, 302.
12. "Letter to Biddy, July 26, 1916," Wheaton College Special Collections Library (SC/122), Chambers papers, series 2, box 17.
13. *Tongues of Fire*, June 1917, Wheaton College Special Collections Library (SC/122), Chambers papers, box 12, folder 6.
14. "Jessop Report, 1917," Wheaton College Special Collections Library (SC/122), Chambers papers, box 8, folder 12.
15. Ibid.
16. Ibid.
17. Chambers, *Oswald Chambers: His Life and Work*, third edition, 279.

## Chapter 10  The Teaching of Adversity

1. Chambers, *My Utmost for His Highest*, August 2.
2. Chambers, "Run Today's Race," *The Complete Works of Oswald Chambers*, 1137.
3. "Kathleen Chambers Interview by David McCasland."
4. Ibid.
5. "Article in *The Life of Faith*, February 17, 1966," Wheaton College Special Collections Library (SC/122), Chambers papers, series 3 (Eva Spink Pulford), box 33, folder 3; misc. articles and clippings.

6. Chambers, "Baffled to Fight Better," *The Complete Works of Oswald Chambers*, 44, 46.

7. Chambers, *Oswald Chambers: His Life and Work*, first edition, 219.

8. Robert Browning, "Asolando," *The Complete Poetic and Dramatic Works of Robert Browning*, Project Gutenberg, accessed March 2, 2017, http://www.gutenberg.org/files/50954/50954-h/50954-h.htm#ASOLANDO.

9. Ashe, "The Book of the Bungalow," 439.

10. "Diary Entry, September 10, 1917," Wheaton College Special Collections Library (SC/122), Chambers papers, series 3, box 21, folder 5.

11. "Jessop Report, 1917."

12. McCasland, *Abandoned to God*, 256.

13. "Jessop Report, 1918," Wheaton College Special Collections Library (SC/122), Chambers papers, box 8, folder 12.

14. *Tongues of Fire*, August 1917, Wheaton College Special Collections Library (SC/122), Chambers papers, box 12, folder 6.

15. McCasland, *Abandoned to God*, 260–61.

16. Ibid., 264–65.

## Chapter 11  What Is That to Thee?

1. Chambers, *My Utmost for His Highest*, November 15.

2. "Kathleen Chambers Interview by David McCasland."

3. "Mary Riley Comments on Oswald Chambers' Death, December 5, 1917," Wheaton College Special Collections Library (SC/122), Chambers papers, series 2, box 17, folder 1.

4. Chambers, *Oswald Chambers: His Life and Work*, first edition, 401.

5. Chambers, *Oswald Chambers: His Life and Work*, second edition, 420.

6. Chambers, "Shade of His Hand," *The Complete Works of Oswald Chambers*, 1236.

7. Chambers, *Oswald Chambers: His Life and Work*, first edition, 401.

8. Fuller story recounted in McCasland, *Abandoned to God*, 275.

9. Ibid., 394.

10. "Biddy Circular Letter to England, December 27, 1917," Wheaton College Special Collections Library (SC/122), Chambers papers, series 2, box 17, folder 1.

11. *Oswald Chambers: His Life and Work*, second edition, 416.

12. "Biddy Circular Letter to England, December 27, 1917."

## Chapter 12  The Fires of Sorrow

1. Chambers, *My Utmost for His Highest*, June 25.

2. "Biddy Circular Letter to England, December 27, 1917."

3. Ibid.

4. Chambers, "The Place of Help," *The Complete Works of Oswald Chambers*, 984.

5. Chambers, *Oswald Chambers: His Life and Work*, second edition, 423.

6. "Letter to Dais and Emily Hobbs, January 5, 1918," Wheaton College Special Collections Library (SC/122), Chambers papers, series 2, box 17, folder 1.

7. "January 12, 1918," Wheaton College Special Collections Library (SC/122), MSS Oswald/Biddy Chambers Diaries/Notebooks, 1902–1919; unprocessed Biddy diary.

8. "January 5, 1918," Wheaton College Special Collections Library (SC/122), MSS Oswald/Biddy Chambers Diaries/Notebooks, 1902–1919; unprocessed Biddy diary.

9. Michael O'Leary, "Part 14: The Wounded and Sick," *The Regimental Rogue: Researching Canadian Soldiers of the First World War*, accessed March 6, 2017, http://regimentalrogue.com/misc/researching_first_world_war_soldiers_part14.htm.

10. "January 21, 1918," Wheaton College Special Collections Library (SC/122), MSS Oswald/Biddy Chambers Diaries/Notebooks, 1902–1919; unprocessed Biddy diary.

11. McCasland, *Abandoned to God*, 278–79.

12. "January 20, 1918," Wheaton College Special Collections Library (SC/122), MSS Oswald/Biddy Chambers Diaries/Notebooks, 1902–1919; unprocessed Biddy diary.

13. "January 23, 1918," Wheaton College Special Collections Library (SC/122), MSS Oswald/Biddy Chambers Diaries/Notebooks, 1902–1919; unprocessed Biddy diary.

14. "1919 YMCA annual report," Wheaton College Special Collections Library (SC/122), Oswald Chambers papers, box 8, folder 12.

15. "June 3, 1918," Wheaton College Special Collections Library (SC/122), MSS Oswald/Biddy Chambers Diaries/Notebooks, 1902–1919; unprocessed Biddy diary.

16. "November 12, 1918," Wheaton College Special Collections Library (SC/122), MSS Oswald/Biddy Chambers Diaries/Notebooks, 1902–1919; unprocessed Biddy diary.

17. "November 15, 1918," Wheaton College Special Collections Library (SC/122), MSS Oswald/Biddy Chambers Diaries/Notebooks, 1902–1919; unprocessed Biddy diary.

18. Following World War I, the wooden crosses that originally marked graves were replaced with a standard headstone so all the graves would look identical, individualized only by name, regiment, death, and religious symbol. It is not known what happened to the carved Bible that originally marked Oswald's grave.

19. Chambers, "Run Today's Race," *The Complete Works of Oswald Chambers*, 1138.

20. "Biddy to Eva Spink, April 8, 1918," Wheaton College Special Collections Library (SC/122), Chambers papers, series 2, box 31, folder 2.

21. "Biddy to 'Tim' Stephen Pulford, April 8, 1918," Wheaton College Special Collections Library (SC/122), Chambers papers, series 2, box 31, folder 2.

22. "The Trip to Jerusalem," Wheaton College Special Collections Library (SC/122), Chambers papers, series 2, box 17, folder 7.

23. Chambers, *Oswald Chambers: His Life and Work*, first edition, 407.

## Chapter 13 Sublime Intimacy

1. Chambers, *My Utmost for His Highest*, August 29.

2. *Spiritual Life*, August 1919, Wheaton College Special Collections Library (SC/122), Chambers papers, box 12, folder 7.

3. "August 25, 1919," Wheaton College Special Collections Library (SC/122), MSS Oswald/Biddy Chambers Diaries/Notebooks, 1902–1919; unprocessed Biddy diary.

4. Ibid.

5. The books remain in print to this day.

6. Chambers, "Our Brilliant Heritage," *The Complete Works of Oswald Chambers*, 940.

7. "August 28, 1918," Wheaton College Special Collections Library (SC/122), MSS Oswald/Biddy Chambers Diaries/Notebooks, 1902–1919; unprocessed Biddy diary.

8. *Training for Cross Cultural Ministries* vol. 2001, no. 1 (March 2001): 1, http://www.contra-mundum.org/schirrmacher/WEFTrainingRoleModel.pdf.

9. Computations taken from MeasuringWorth.com, https://www.measuring worth.com/calculators/exchange/result_exchange.php.

10. "Stephen Pulford Letter, August 27, 1968," Wheaton College Special Collections Library (SC/122), Chambers papers, series 8 (Kathleen Chambers), box 54, folder 1.

11. "October 9, 1919," Wheaton College Special Collections Library (SC/122), MSS Oswald/Biddy Chambers Diaries/Notebooks, 1902–1919; unprocessed Biddy diary.

12. "Kathleen Chambers Interview by David McCasland."

13. "December 9, 1919," Wheaton College Special Collections Library (SC/122), MSS Oswald/Biddy Chambers Diaries/Notebooks, 1902–1919; unprocessed Biddy diary.

14. Ibid., "September 3, 1919."

15. "Kathleen Chambers Interview by David McCasland."

16. Pamela, "The Great Silence," *History in the Margins*, November 11, 2013, http://www.historyinthemargins.com/2013/11/11/the-great-silence.

17. "November 11, 1919," Wheaton College Special Collections Library (SC/122), MSS Oswald/Biddy Chambers Diaries/Notebooks, 1902–1919; unprocessed Biddy diary.

18. *The Life of Faith*, February 17, 1966, Wheaton College Special Collections Library (SC/122), Chambers papers, series 3, box 33, folder 3; misc. articles and clippings.

19. "Kathleen Chambers Interview by David McCasland."

20. Ibid.

21. Chambers, *Oswald Chambers: His Life and Work*, first edition, 279.

22. "Kathleen Chambers Interview by David McCasland."

23. "The Inter-War Years: 1918–1939," *Striking Women*, accessed March 6, 2017, http://www.striking-women.org/module/women-and-work/inter-war -years-1918-1939.

### Chapter 14 Isn't There Some Misunderstanding?

1. Chambers, *My Utmost for His Highest*, March 28.

2. "Oswald to Biddy, September 17, 1916," Wheaton College Special Collections Library (SC/122), Chambers papers, box 1, folder 12.

3. "Kathleen Chambers Interview by David McCasland."

4. "Kathleen Chambers Interview by David McCasland"; see also Mary Wesley, "Recollections of a Childhood in Yarnton in the Early Years of the Twentieth Century," Yarnton Village—The Community Website for Yarnton Village, September 1999, http://www.yarnton-village.org.uk/recollections-of-childhood/.

5. Chambers, *My Utmost for His Highest*, November 7.

6. "Kathleen Chambers Interview by David McCasland."

7. Chambers, "Shade of His Hand," *The Complete Works of Oswald Chambers*, 1192.

8. "Kathleen Chambers Interview by David McCasland."

9. Ibid.

10. Ibid.

11. Chambers, *My Utmost for His Highest*, January 11.

12. "Kathleen Chambers Interview by David McCasland."

13. "Oswald to Biddy, September 1, 1916," Wheaton College Special Collections Library (SC/122), Chambers papers, box 9, folder 2.

14. "Kathleen Chambers Interview by David McCasland."

15. Ibid.

16. Ibid.

17. Ibid.

18. Ibid.

19. Brother Francis SSF, "Brother Douglas Downes," *The Society of St. Francis: Province of the Divine Compassion*, accessed March 6, 2017, http://www.franciscan.org.au/2003/03/04/brother-douglas-downes/.

20. Chambers, *My Utmost for His Highest*, foreword.

21. Chambers, "The Pilgrim's Song Book," *The Complete Works of Oswald Chambers*, 530.

22. "Kathleen Chambers Interview by David McCasland."

23. Ibid.

## Chapter 15 The Worker's Ruling Passion

1. Chambers, *My Utmost for His Highest*, March 27.

2. "Kathleen Chambers Interview by David McCasland."

3. Ibid.

4. "Kathleen Chambers Interview by David McCasland." Kathleen recounted two different stories about boarding school. She told Chambers biographer David McCasland she attended the Dollar School in Scotland. Elsewhere, Kathleen said she attended boarding school in Eastbourne, a popular spot for boarding schools on the southeastern coast of England. Her paternal aunt Bertha Chambers ran a lodging house in the town, and Kathleen spent weekends with her. Records at the Dollar School burned and were unavailable for verification; therefore, where Kathleen attended boarding school is unconfirmed.

5. "Kathleen Chambers Interview by David McCasland"; see also "Bermondsey Medical Mission Hospital for Women and Children," *Lost Hospitals of London*, accessed March 6, 2017, http://ezitis.myzen.co.uk/bermondsey70.html.

6. "Kathleen Chambers Interview by David McCasland."

7. Chambers, "Not Knowing Whither," *The Complete Works of Oswald Chambers*, 863.

8. *BTC Monthly Journal*, November 1940, Wheaton College Special Collections Library (SC/122), Chambers papers, box 14, folder 8.

9. *BTC Monthly Journal*, 1932–1933, Wheaton College Special Collections Library (SC/122), Chambers papers, box 14, folder 2.

10. Diana Athill, *Stet* (New York: Grove Press, 2002), 43.

11. Chambers, *Oswald Chambers: His Life and Work*, first edition, 9.

12. Ibid., 10.

13. "Kathleen Chambers Interview by David McCasland."

14. Ibid.

15. Article in *The Life of Faith*, February 17, 1966, Wheaton College Special Collections Library (SC/122), Chambers papers, series 3 (Eva Spink Pulford), box 33, folder 3.

16. "OCPA Minutes, June 1934," Wheaton College Special Collections Library (SC/122), Chambers papers, series 4 (Oswald Chambers Publications Association), box 36, folder 1.

17. "OCPA Minutes, June 1936," Wheaton College Special Collections Library (SC/122), Chambers papers, series 4, box 36, folder 1.

18. "Kathleen Chambers Interview by David McCasland."

19. Ibid.

20. Ibid.

21. Ibid.

22. Ibid.

23. Ibid.

## Chapter 16 The Teaching of Adversity

1. Chambers, *My Utmost for His Highest*, August 2.

2. Chambers, "The Pilgrim's Song Book," *The Complete Works of Oswald Chambers*, 525.

3. Ibid., 526.

4. Computations taken from MeasuringWorth.com, https://www.measuring worth.com/calculators/exchange/result_exchange.php.

5. *The Bookseller*, September 7, 1939, as quoted in Valerie Holman, *Print for Victory* (London: The British Library, 2008), 15.

6. "OCPA Minutes, July 1940," Wheaton College Special Collections Library (SC/122), Chambers papers, series 4, box 36, folder 1.

7. Biddy's personal copy of *Thine Is the Kingdom: A Book of Prayers for Use in Time of War* by Canon Normal H. Clarke, Wheaton College Special Collections Library (SC/122), Chambers papers, series 2, box 19.

8. "Kathleen Chambers Interview by David McCasland."

9. Ibid.

10. "Biddy to Eva Spink Pulford, circa September 1940," Wheaton College Special Collections Library (SC/122), Chambers papers, series 3, box 22, folder 4.

11. "Peterel," *The Bookseller*, January 2, 1941, as quoted in Holman, *Print for Victory*, 30.

12. "Kathleen Chambers Interview by David McCasland."

13. Ibid.

14. Holman, *Print for Victory*, 271.

15. "OCPA Minutes, October 1942," Wheaton College Special Collections Library (SC/122), Chambers papers, series 4, box 36.

16. Computations taken from MeasuringWorth.com, https://www.measuring worth.com/calculators/exchange/result_exchange.php.

17. "Kathleen Chambers Interview by David McCasland."

18. "Testimony of a Missionary Recruit," *BTC Monthly Journal*, post-1946 edition, 63, Wheaton College Special Collections Library (SC/122), Chambers papers, box 15, folder 9.

19. *BTC Monthly Journal*, August 1945, Wheaton College Special Collections Library (SC/122), Chambers papers, box 14, folder 4.

## Chapter 17 Yes—But . . . !

1. Chambers, *My Utmost for His Highest*, May 30.

2. Farley Mowat, *Aftermath Travels in a Post-War World* (Lanham, MD: Roberts Rinehart, 1996), 6.

3. "Hittle Letter, 1957," Wheaton College Special Collections Library (SC/122), Chambers papers, box 6, folder 8.

4. *BTC Monthly Journal*, November 1940, 34/40, Wheaton College Special Collections Library (SC/122), Chambers papers, series 4, box 36, folder 1.

5. Ibid., 1.

6. "Biddy to Eva, April 1951," Wheaton College Special Collections Library (SC/122), Chambers papers, series 3, box 22, folder 4.

7. *BTC Monthly Journal*, April 1952, Wheaton College Special Collections Library (SC/122), Chambers papers, box 15, folder 11.

8. "Kathleen Chambers Interview by David McCasland."

9. Ibid.

10. Ibid.

11. Ibid.

12. Ibid.

13. Ibid.

14. By 1967, 50 percent of UK remains were cremated. See Daniel J. Davis, *Death, Ritual, and Belief: The Rhetoric of Funerary Rites* (London: Bloomsbury Publishing, 2002), 28.

15. "Kathleen Chambers Interview by David McCasland."

16. Ibid.

17. Martha Christian, *Searching for Mrs. Oswald Chambers* (Carol Stream, IL: Tyndale, 2008), ebook.

18. Author conversation with Christopher Pulford, October 6, 2016.

19. Author conversation with Ian Pulford, October 6, 2016.

20. Brother Andrew and Verne Becker, *For the Love of My Brothers* (Minneapolis, Bethany: 1998), 30.

## Chapter 18 Undaunted Radiance

1. Chambers, *My Utmost for His Highest*, March 7.
2. Chambers, "Run Today's Race," *The Complete Works of Oswald Chambers*, 1157.
3. Author conversation with David McCasland, August 25, 2016.
4. Ibid.
5. "Kathleen Chambers Interview by David McCasland."
6. Ibid.
7. *Notes to Kathleen*, Wheaton College Special Collections Library (SC/122), Chambers papers, series 8 (Kathleen Chambers), box 54, folder 1.
8. "OCPA Minutes, October 31, 1964," Wheaton College Special Collections Library (SC/122), Chambers papers, series 4, box 36, folder 2.
9. *Notes to Kathleen*.
10. "Eva's Diaries, January 15–20, 1966, 1967, 1968, 1972," Wheaton College Special Collections Library (SC/122), Chambers papers, series 3, box 28, folders 13–15.
11. Ibid.
12. Author email with Minal Patel, Marylebone crematorium supervisor, November 23, 2016; see also "St. Marylebone Crematorium—Memorials," accessed March 6, 2017, http://www.thelondoncremation.co.uk/st-marylebone-cremator ium/memorials/.
13. "Undated Letter to Eva Spink Pulford, circa 1972," Wheaton College Special Collections Library (SC/122), Chambers papers, series 8, box 54, folder 1.
14. Author email with Brother Andrew, May 23, 2016.
15. Author email with Os Guinness, April 25, 2016.
16. "Kathleen Chambers Interview by David McCasland."
17. Article in *The Life of Faith*, February 17, 1966, Wheaton College Special Collections Library (SC/122), Chambers papers, series 3, box 33, folder 3.
18. Ibid.

## Appendix Biddy Chambers and the Writing of *My Utmost for His Highest*, 1924–27

1. Author conversation with Dr. Jed Macosko, June 16, 2016.
2. Chambers, *My Utmost for His Highest*, foreword.
3. Dr. Ken Boa, *Themes in My Utmost for His Highest*, Breakpoint's Great Books CD series, no. 18, produced circa 2007.

# Bibliography

## Oswald and Biddy Chambers

Chambers, B. *Oswald Chambers: His Life and Work*, first, second, and third editions. London: Simpkin Marshall, 1933, 1938, 1959.

Chambers, Oswald. *My Utmost for His Highest*, classic edition. Uhrichsville, OH: Barbour Publishing, 1963 (also the online version: www.utmost.org).

———. *The Complete Works of Oswald Chambers*. Grand Rapids: Discovery House, 2000. Includes a CD/DVD featuring a 1991 interview with Kathleen Chambers conducted by David McCasland.

Christian, Martha. *Searching for Mrs. Oswald Chambers*. Carol Stream, IL: Tyndale House Publishers, 2008.

Lambert, D. L. *Oswald Chambers: An Unbribed Soul*. London: Oswald Chambers Publications Association, 1968.

Macosko, Dr. Jed and Dr. Cecilie Macosko. *A Daily Companion to My Utmost for His Highest*. Grand Rapids: Discovery House, 2014.

McCasland, David. *Oswald Chambers: Abandoned to God*. Grand Rapids: Discovery House, 1993.

## General

Andrew, Brother. *God's Smuggler*. Grand Rapids: Chosen Books, 1967.

Andrew, Brother with Verne Becker. *For the Love of My Brothers*. Minneapolis: Bethany, 1998.

Ashe, Katherine. *The Book of the College*. London: Ballantyne Press, circa 1915.

Athill, Diana. *Stet*. New York: Grove Press, 2002.

Bilton, David. *Hull Pals: 10th, 11th, 12th and 13th Battalions East Yorkshire Regiment*. South Yorkshire: Pen and Sword, 2014.

Cowman, L. B. *Streams in the Desert*. Grand Rapids: Zondervan, 1997.

*Daily Light on the Daily Path*. Grand Rapids: Zondervan, 1981.

Davis, Daniel J. *Death, Ritual, and Belief: The Rhetoric of Funerary Rites*. London: Bloomsbury Publishing, 2002.

Holman, Valerie. *Print for Victory: Book Publishing in England 1939–1945*. London: The British Library, 2008.

Mowat, Farley. *Aftermath: Travels in a Post-War World*. Lanham, MD: Roberts Rinehart Publishers, 1996.

VanEmden, Richard. *The Quick and the Dead*. London: Bloomsbury Publishing, 2011.

## Non-Book Resources

Boa, Dr. Ken. *Themes from My Utmost for His Highest*. Audio CD no. 18, The Great Books Audio CD series. Produced by Breakpoint, circa 2007. Content available at http://www.kenboa.org/shop/my-utmost-for-his-highest-oswald-chambers/.

Chambers family tree (www.ancestry.com), developed by the author: http://trees.ancestry.com/tree/80748053/family. Public or research libraries may have access to Ancestry.com, a subscription service.

Oswald Chambers Publications Association, Ltd. http://www.oswald chambers.co.uk/bio/.

# About the Author

Longtime Bible study teacher and genealogist Michelle Ule is the bestselling author of seven published works. An English literature graduate of the University of California, Los Angeles, and a "retired" Navy wife, she lives in Northern California with her terrific family.

For more information about her and to read all her blog posts about Oswald and Biddy Chambers, visit her website at www.michelleule.com.

# Meet Michelle!

To learn more about Michelle's
writing and speaking, visit
**MICHELLEULE.COM**

MichelleUle

MichelleUleWriter

MichelleUle